√ 6.50

Television Drama: An Introduction

Television Drama: An Introduction

David Self

MACMILLAN

© David Self 1984

First published 1984
Reprinted 1986

Published by
MACMILLAN EDUCATION LTD
Houndmills, Basingstoke, Hampshire RG21 2XS
and London
Companies and representatives
throughout the world

Filmsetting by Vantage Photosetting Co. Ltd
Eastleigh and London

Printed in Hong Kong

British Library Cataloguing in Publication Data
Self, David
Television drama.
1. Television plays   2. Television-
Production and direction
I. Title
791.45'75   PN1992.65
ISBN 0-333-36611-5
ISBN 0-333-36612-3 (Pbk)

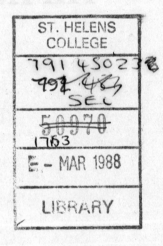

Contents

List of Plates

Acknowledgements

No one who has read Shaun Sutton's *The Largest Theatre in the World* or Frank Pike's collection of essays *Ah! Mischief*, and who then writes about television drama can be other than deeply indebted to them, and the author acknowledges his debt to them and to many friends and colleagues in Anglia Television, the BBC and the Society of Authors; and in particular to Maggie McPherson and Edward Kelsey. He is also aware that, although television is in many ways a male-dominated industry, both men and women make significant contributions in all departments and hopes that where pronouns indicate one gender, they will not be taken as excluding the other.

The author and publishers should like to thank Oriel Press for permission to reproduce p. 2 of Cecil P. Taylor's play *Charles and Cromwell* which appears in Cecil P. Taylor's *Making a TV Play* (1970).

Preface

Once upon a time, drama was a way of honouring the gods. Pilgrims made their way to Epidavros or to Delphi in order to witness performances that retold the stories of their heroes, human and divine. In a later age, drama was not so much an act of worship, more a luxury. By carriage or cab, the selected few could travel to town 'to see a show'. Later still, at a flick of a switch in every living-room, anyone could view the entire *Oresteia* or the latest social comedy. Better still, many could record them and watch them at a time best suited to the individual.

In the words of Raymond Williams, Professor of Drama at Cambridge, Britain had become 'a dramatised society', with drama a daily and domestic experience. Now, most people watch many hours a week, as a seemingly inexhaustible supply streams into each home: *Crossroads, Brideshead Revisited, Minder, Measure for Measure*. . . . Seventeen million people watch a single episode of the twice-weekly *Coronation Street*. Four million watch a Shakespeare play on one Sunday evening. (It takes the Royal Shakespeare Company four years, playing in all its theatres, to play to that size of audience.)

At the time of writing, Britain has not yet experienced cable television (apart from a few small-scale experiments). When that comes, with its multiplicity of channels, and when direct broadcasting by satellite begins, one might expect an even richer diet of drama. However, there are those who believe that the golden age of television drama is already over and that the future will see not an expansion of the drama output but a retraction. 'Within a matter of years, two of the four great

resources of British broadcasting will have vanished: writing
and acting. Only music and the visual arts will remain.' Such
was the gloomy prediction of Michael Kuhn, an authority on
cable television, at the 1983 Edinburgh Television Festival.
Indeed, as I write, there is every indication that cable television will consist mainly of popular music, feature films and
sport. Few cable operators will wish to invest in expensive
drama production. If they attract as much of the audience as
they expect to (so the argument goes), then sooner or later
neither the BBC nor the Independent Television network
companies will be able to justify or afford the production of
original drama.

But this book is not intended as an obituary. It is written in
the hope that diversity and quality will be maintained and
developed, though its primary purpose is to record the state
and the practice of the art of television drama as television
enters a new age of multi-channel distribution.

Because the extent of television drama is even now so
enormous, it has been necessary to impose some limits on the
scope of a book of this size. It is restricted to descriptions of
British practice and (despite the excellent writing, acting and
direction to be seen in such a series as *A Fine Romance*) it does
not cover programmes generally labelled as 'comedy' or 'situation comedy'. Nor does it cover films made for the cinema,
even though they form a significant proportion of the drama to
be seen on television.

To many, television drama is a mystique. Many of those
involved in it professionally labour to keep it that way.
Technicians talk in an almost impenetrable jargon. Directors
speak patronisingly to those 'who just don't understand its
grammar'. 'Of course,' they say, 'when you've been in the
game as long as I have, then you'll understand!' (Five years
earlier, their experience of direction was limited to a university
drama society and a fringe theatre in outer Edinburgh.)
Academics also maintain the mystery. With talk of 'authorial
ideologies', 'the interplay of inter-related discourses' and
'textual codes', they pontificate upon a Cockney thriller that
was constructed with one simple aim in mind: to get high
ratings.

This book's secondary aim therefore is to penetrate the

mystique and clarify the process by which a television drama is made. It is intended as a primer for students of television, both those on courses which are mainly critical or theoretical and those on courses which include a practical element but where resources preclude the production and recording of a full-scale play.

It is also intended for the general reader and student of related disciplines in the hope that it will increase the appreciation of a particularly strange art form: a form created not by an individual but by a team working within a highly competitive manufacturing industry.

INTRODUCTORY NOTE TO REPRINT

The typescript of this book was completed in December 1983, since when there have been such notable productions as Granada Television's adaptation of Paul Scott's *Jewel in the Crown;* and something of a resurgence within the drama department of the BBC. In particular there has been the Corporation's highly successful re-entry into the world of 'soap' with its strongly scripted, twice-weekly *EastEnders;* and there has also been its much acclaimed thriller serial, *Edge of Darkness.*

Otherwise the state of television drama at the start of 1986 is largely as described in this book, but with an increasing number of co-productions in the pipeline and more use of one- or two-camera video units on location. However, with the Peacock Committee about to report on the future of the BBC and with the ITV franchises coming up for renewal, British television could soon undergo a period of change. Already there are demands that programme makers should be more 'responsible' and 'accountable' – demands which some see as nannyish restraints on the creative process.

David Self

February, 1986

1.

Genres and Media

One particularly depressing sound still to be heard in the land is the English don who, while lecturing on Shakespeare as a truly popular dramatist whose plays could pack the Globe any afternoon, scorns television drama simply because it caters for a mass audience. Yet it is probable that more people see a single transmission of a television play than saw all of Shakespeare's plays during his lifetime. Similarly, a modern drama must fill a theatre six nights a week for many years in order to equal the average audience of a 'Play for Today'.

No wonder then that modern dramatists, such as Dennis Potter, see television drama as an important medium:

> There in the middle of the news bulletins, the ads, the sports, entertainments and party politicals, there in virtually every home in the land, seen with the social guard down and the texture of the modern world all around it, is a precious space for *drama*: the great playwrights of the past would surely have sought to use this medium to address their fellow citizens.

This points to one of the attractions of the television play. It allows the writer the chance to present his 'message' to an enormous audience in a way that is quite impossible in the theatre, and in no other genre of television drama has the writer (and production team) more freedom than in the so-called 'single play'. Perhaps this is why the television dramatist Hugh Whitemore sees 'a remarkably rigid structure of class distinctions' within television drama:

At the top are the aristocrats of the single play, then come those who work on prestige serials, followed by the manufacturers of popular series, with soap opera labourers languishing at the bottom. Somewhere in the middle – the equivalent of skilled plumbers, perhaps, or electrical engineers – are those who make dramatizations and adaptations.[1]

In this introductory chapter, in which we shall consider the various genres of television drama and the various media in which they can be made, it therefore seems only right to begin with the product of the aristocrats.

The Single Play

The single play is complete in itself. It is not part of a series (although it may be advertised under a generic or 'banner' title such as 'Armchair Theatre' or 'Play for Today'. It does not have to conform to a given format or involve existing characters. It can in theory be of any length. It will gain critical attention. It will be an 'event' within the ceaseless schedules. Most of all, it gives writers, directors and designers an empty screen on which to be original, imaginative and provocative. However, there are limits to such artistic freedom, as the critic and practitioner W. Stephen Gilbert indicates:

> Clearly what it is possible for a one-off play to do is heavily circumscribed by company policy (budgetary provision, length and timing of transmission), by conscious or subconscious observation of televisual conventions, both of form and of the 'messages' contained in the work. Nonetheless, the play remains an atypical piece of television. The company which produces it does not, except in very rare circumstances, expect it to generate further programmes. It is understood that the material will be broadcast once (or, happily, twice; or, if it wins prizes, thrice) and that thereafter none of its components will be pursued – its characters, its *mise en scène*, its themes or its particular combination of actors, director, writer and production team.[2]

No wonder then, despite the critical acclaim that may accrue to a production company following a successful single play, that the form does not automatically commend itself to managements and accountants. It is expensive. It needs far more planning and rehearsal time than an episode within a series or serial. It requires special scenery and costumes. It cannot be sold to overseas markets as readily or as profitably as a series. (Think of the sales manager visiting an international television festival in Cannes, Montreux or Acapulco, vaguely trying to justify his flight, champagne and caviare. Will he endear himself more to his company back in Birmingham if he sells one eighty-minute social drama or twenty-six episodes of a police thriller?) Nor, if the play is to be transmitted on a commercial channel, will it appeal as much as a series to an advertising-campaign manager.

'My client likes to know where he's advertising. This slot in the middle of "Drama of Tomorrow". . . . What's that series all about?'

'Well, it's not a series. They're all single plays.'

'You mean, all different?'

'Yes, one might be a farce, another about Northern Ireland.'

'Forget it.'

More surprisingly, the single play does not always delight the viewer, as W. Stephen Gilbert again points out:

The teleplay is a rude shock to this cosy system. Nothing in tonight's teleplay will guarantee you anything about next week's production. If you miss it, you will not be able to 'catch up' next week. Moreover, because its characters and its themes will be unique to it, you will find yourself launched on unfamiliar territory. You may even be confronted with a style – of dialogue, of story-telling, of filming, of design, of acting – which is unfamiliar. It is this unfamiliarity which leads a certain kind of viewer to declare that he or she 'does not like' television plays. Upon examination, this position is readily reduced to the true state of affairs: that the viewer does not *watch* television plays; it is the unfamiliarity that is not liked and hence is avoided.

All the more credit is due then to the managements which

have nurtured the single play when it has attracted audiences which, while large in theatrical terms, are only moderate when measured on a television scale and in relation to the investment of plant and cash. Indeed, the single play (a particularly British phenomenon and one of the glories of British television) has often seemed to be above the commercial strictures that programme controllers apply to other types as television. As Graham Murdock observed (while researching at the Centre for Mass Communication Research, Leicester),

> In contrast to series, single plays are not in the front line of the export drive or of the domestic ratings battle. Consequently they are to a large extent exempt from direct market pressures. They are not required to accommodate themselves to dominant currents within popular consciousness or to work within the prevailing ethos of entertainment. On the contrary, they are expected to operate with the ideology of creativity. Hence, where series writers are nudged towards the articulation of general ideologies, playwrights are explicitly encouraged to express their own preoccupations and commitments. As a result, single plays are one of the few areas within modern television where emergent themes and unorthodox or oppositional views can be presented and worked through. This notion that creativity carries with it a licence to provoke is built into the institutional ideology which broadcasting has taken over from the art world.[3]

This freedom to be 'different' can perhaps be illustrated by a play shown in 1979 in BBC-1's 'Play for Today' slot. Called *Coming Out*, it was written by James Andrew Hall. It did not prove to be a 'famous' play; it was not 'brilliant'. It was more than merely 'good' and it illustrated a particular merit of the single play, as defined by one of the producers of 'Play for Today', Kenith Trodd: 'I don't think anyone now believes that you can change the world by television. But you can inch it, edge it. . . .' *Coming Out* was reviewed in *The Listener* by Peter Buckman:

> *Coming Out* attempted something altogether more serious, to question whether a homosexual's private life is his own

affair, or whether he owes it to the gay community to declare himself. Anton Rodgers played Lewis Duncan, a bestselling author of tough thrillers, who is persuaded by a magazine editor (boyishly played by Hywel Bennett) to write a pseudonymous article exhorting gays to be neither ashamed nor tediously declamatory. The reaction to this article intrudes on his privacy, and the indiscretion of his lover destroys their longstanding affair. This pushes Lewis into 'coming out': he declares himself to a virtual stranger, who splutters with outrage, but does no more about it than Lewis seems prepared to do. Nothing resolved, then, but a few attitudes aired, which is what Kenith Trodd must have meant when he talked of 'inching' the public towards coming to terms with the problems raised by the drama.[4]

In the same month of April 1979 in which *Coming Out* was first transmitted, London Weekend Television devoted an edition of its arts-magazine programme, *The South Bank Show*, to an enquiry into 'The Rise and Fall of the Single Play'. It reflected a widespread feeling that the charmed life of the single play was threatened and a conviction that its heyday was over. LWT's survey included clips from plays shown in its 'golden age' (the 1960s and 1970s) which illustrated how techniques had changed from an almost theatrical presentation with static cameras and long shots to the employment of rapid cutting and telling use of close-ups. For those who had watched the plays on transmission it brought back potent memories of the rich fare on offer then. Plays by David Mercer (*Where the Difference Begins, A Suitable Case for Treatment* and *The Buried Man*), by Peter Nichols (*A Walk on the Grass, When the Wind Blows* and *The Gorge*) and many more by John Mortimer, Alun Owen, John Hopkins and David Turner came back to mind from the sixties. We realised the seventies had been equally rich, at least so far as the BBC's output had been concerned. As its then head of drama, Shaun Sutton, has catalogued in another place,

So abundant were the seventies, I can only dip in at random and bring out *Elizabeth R*, John Bowen's *Robin Redbreast*, Peter Nichols' *Hearts and Flowers*, Ingmar Bergmann's *The Lie*, Jeremy Sandford's *Edna the Inebriate Woman*,

Tom Clarke's *Stocker's Copper*, *The Wessex Tales*, Colin Welland's *Kisses at Fifty* and *Leeds – United!* There was Arthur Hopcraft's *The Reporters*, Dennis Potter's *Joe's Ark* and *Blue Remembered Hills*, John McGrath's *The Cheviot, The Stag, and the Black Black Oil*, Peter McDougall's *Just Another Saturday*, David Hare's *Licking Hitler*, David Mercer's *Shooting the Chandelier*, Trevor Griffiths' *Through the Night*, Frederick Raphael's *The Glittering Prizes*, John Hopkins' *A Story to Frighten the Children*, Hugh Whitemore's *84 Charing Cross Road*, Jack Rosenthal's *Spend Spend Spend*, Jim Allen's *The Spongers*, G. F. Newman's *Law and Order* and *Billy*.[5]

In one year (1973) taken at random from that decade, there were twenty-eight 'Plays for Today' on BBC-1, and on BBC-2 about the same number of 'Thirty Minute Theatre' and half a dozen seventy-five- or ninety-minute plays. This rate of production did not fall significantly in the subsequent four or five years, though there were fewer half-hour plays than formerly.

In contrast, in the early seventies, the single play went into something of a decline on the ITV network. One argument at first put forward by the production companies was that they simply could not afford to make this kind of play; yet even in the mid and late seventies, when their profits were considerable, the single play was still a rarity. Less than a quarter of the number of genuinely original single television plays was being produced by the ITV companies in 1979 than had been produced fifteen years earlier.

One producer, Barry Hanson, interviewed in 'The Rise and Fall of the Single Play', indicated that the pressure was not entirely financial and that the needs of the television publicist (like those of the advertiser) were involved:

People want packages. If you were to go to the press office in a television company and you were to say, 'I've got these single plays', they'd say, 'What are they about?' You'd say, 'They're about this and about that, they're single plays.' You see, the pressure is to work on a theme, so that people can say, 'It's about this. I know what it's about and that's what I'm going to see.' With individual work, coming from wherever, you can't do that . . . and that is anathema to anybody who wants to get neat packages scheduled everywhere.[6]

At the same time, television writers (such as Robert Holles) were arguing their own interests:

The single play provides an entry into television for talented young dramatists, whether they come from fringe theatre, radio drama, or any other source. Over the last twenty years, it would be no exaggeration to say that eighty per cent of the television dramatists now working on drama series, serials, and adaptations made their original break-through, and learned their trade, through the medium of the single play. If the single play was to disappear, where would these talented professional dramatists come from? Advertising copy-writers perhaps?

Furthermore, television dramatists who are now largely involved in working on drama series need an escape route into a single play market in order to refresh their imaginations, which cannot be exercised by continually writing to a format with established characters.[7]

Many producers and even some managements would acknowledge the validity of Robert Holles's arguments. Even if budgets are not immediately forthcoming as a result, there is still at least a theoretical awareness that, without the opportunity for innovation, television drama could become as bland and as stale in this country as it has in others. An appreciation of this need to encourage new ideas and new talent was expressed in an article which appeared in the 1980 edition of the IBA's official handbook, *Television and Radio*. Beginning with a commitment that 'the single play is an important element of television drama and it must remain so', it went on to quote David Reid, then head of drama at ATV:

The perplexing aspect for audience and practitioner alike is that by their very nature single plays cover the whole spectrum of content and style. There can be no rules, only guidelines. Television plays must be allowed to range from

farce to tragedy and so we must take risks and, in conse-
quence, sometimes we fail. The successes, however, are an
investment for the future, since more often than not they
force us to question what we are doing in all other areas of
drama – and that prevents us from becoming complacent
and losing touch with our audience.[8]

Just how much in touch the makers of the television play are
with their audience is a question for a later chapter. It is
enough to note here that one of the most distinguished of
television playwrights, Dennis Potter, has felt little contact
with his viewers:

There is no tension crackling back across the footlights from
the unseen audience, little sense of expectation, no vivifying
tradition of great work, and only the scantiest of evidence
that the bulk of its 'viewers' (oh, passive noun!) consider it a
finer or deeper experience than any other sort of moving
picture.

Sadly, when the viewer's voice was actually heard during
that 'golden age' we have been considering, it was often (and
certainly according to sections of the popular press) protesting
vigorously against 'kitchen sink' dramas, 'plays without
proper endings' and depravity. There were even periods when
'The Wednesday Play' and 'Play for Today' were phrases that
could raise a cheap laugh, so closely had they become identified in the public's mind with 'smut'. Nevertheless, those
same plays (and others which won a more positive response)
did 'inch' the public conscience; and (in retrospect, quite
amazingly) the BBC and some ITV companies did preserve the
genre. Now, with the growth of independent producers, the
merging of film and television techniques, and the public's
new readiness to accept longer plays, the future of the single
play seems more assured than when London Weekend chronicled its decline. That is obviously healthy for the industry and
encouraging for those who care that television should be a
creative medium. It is also healthy for the public at large, as
writer and producer John Bowen has written:

From early times, questions of right and wrong behaviour, have been presented and discussed in stories. The stories have taken different forms both between cultures and within cultures, and they still do. In Britain and most of the industrialized countries, a majority of the population does not read novels, never goes to the theatre and seldom to the cinema; the appetite for stories remains, and must be satisfied by television. Those artists who are story-tellers – who perform that necessary task in society – must therefore have access to television, and not just at its fringes. They should be helped to speak to as many as will listen – moral ideas are not confined to an élite in a healthy society. They, in return, should not make private art in a public place. There is a responsibility however complex the ideas, to be accessible. There is a responsibility to tell a story. However much television's administrators may believe (on inadequate evidence) that the public does not like plays, and anyway series and serials are more controllable, however much ambitious and underpaid writers may wish to be commissioned to write 'television novels', the single play must be the main source of such stories. . . . Experienced writers must be allowed sometimes to tread water, new writers to try out a voice, and above all the public to become accustomed to the regular exercise of judgment and empathy.[9]

Theatre Plays

In what has been called the 'first age' of television (that is, the period up to the mid fifties) much of the drama output was of stage plays more or less adapted for the new medium. Before the war, there was a regular programme, *Theatre Parade*, which presented studio excerpts from current West End hits, rather as a modern cinema programme trails 'clips' from new releases. Even into the late fifties, there were occasional live transmissions from London theatres of plays then in production. Bizarrely, these presentations were frequently of only the second act. With cameras confined to preordained positions with little opportunity for close-ups and with an audience present, the result was often formal, stylised and (in the worst sense) theatrical.

There are critics and practitioners who would say that, no matter what technical tricks you play, a stage play is always a stage play and cannot be made into television drama. They will point out that it is conceived in a different way, it is structured in lengthy and slow-moving acts and not in neatly intercut scenes, and that it is wordy rather than visual. They will stress that a stage play cannot be 'good' (equalling original) television, or that any television screening is a poor substitute for a theatrical event. It must be admitted that some plays are simply not 'televisual'. Television is certainly happier with the intimate than with the epic. It conveys realism more easily than the symbolic or impressionistic. It is not a natural medium for pageant. All that said, even large-scale stage plays can work and have worked most successfully on the small screen. There have also been those occasions when they have failed singularly: when directors have treated texts with too much reverence or when they have swamped them with unnecessary images.

Of course, at one level, television (or at least video tape) is simply a very useful way of preserving for posterity a notable stage production. For example, in 1982, the National Theatre staged a highly acclaimed production of *The Oresteia*, the trilogy by Aeschylus. An all-male cast playing in classical masks on an ash- and sand-coloured set re-created the epic story of Agamemnon's return home from the Trojan Wars, his murder, and of how his son Orestes avenges his death. It played to packed houses and could have run for many more performances than were possible. The National Theatre was invited by Channel 4 to record the production and it was shown on that network in 1983. Like the stage production, the television version was directed by Peter Hall, being recorded during public performances. From the director's box at the back of the Olivier Theatre (the National Theatre auditorium in which it was given), Peter Hall talked to the four cameramen over four performances as if they were covering a football match. 'There was no shooting script. I'd say, "Shoot what interests you. You're free."' If the television production lacked the grandeur of the original, it had its own rhythms as cameras cut from mask to mask in the tableaux. It conveyed urgency, fear and excitement. It proved to be more than a record of an evening in the theatre: it worked acceptably as television.

Another National Theatre production transferred even more successfully to the small screen some years earlier. Eduardo de Filippo's *Saturday, Sunday, Monday* is a traditional three-act play, a comic melodrama set in an Italian household. The theatre production had been strong on realism, including genuine cooking on stage. The domestic setting moved comfortably into the studio and, although the characters are excitable Italians in a state of crisis, the performances needed less scaling-down for television than do many stage roles. It is in fact a play which might equally well have been conceived as a television play. For all these reasons, its transfer to television proved particularly happy. It also served indirectly as an indicator that many other stage productions have been televised simply because they were successes in the theatre, and without due thought being given to such questions as whether they were of a scale and pace suitable for television and what would need doing to them before they would be as effective on the screen as on the stage.

Due thought was given to the transfer of a production potentially quite unsuited to television. *The Wars of the Roses* had been a hit for the Royal Shakespeare Company in the mid sixties. It was a trilogy of full-length plays adapted from the three parts of Shakespeare's *Henry VI* and from *Richard III*, a 'wide screen' production if ever there was one. Yet the BBC Television Drama Group felt it was so important and impressive an achievement that it should be brought to the 'millions who could not crowd into the theatre at Stratford-upon-Avon and to audiences overseas in Canada and the USA'. Michael Bakewell has described the process by which the stage version was turned into television drama, recorded on location in the theatre (see also p. 120):

The central problem of production was to re-create fully as possible the experience felt by the audience watching the plays at Stratford and it soon became apparent that this could not be done simply by slavishly photographing the action. Theatre has its own grammar and television another. They are involved in different concepts of reality and illusion. One of the great features of the Stratford production was the movement of the set itself: the periactoid swung round to become at one moment the walls of Har- fleur, at another the council-chamber in London: the back- ground grilles would fly up and the great throne would be trundled forward; the council-chamber would rise up from its slot in the fore-stage—none of this, it was realised, would work on television. This was partly a question of reality, but more so one of tempo. A television audience comes to accept, automatically, the cut, the mix, the fade to black as traditional methods of getting from scene to scene, and the ingenious movements of John Bury's set would, in the end, have become merely tedious.[10]

Inevitably, and correctly, the television version moved to- wards a realism impossible in a normal theatrical run:

The Duke of Burgundy rode in on a horse, Clarence really was dunked in a butt (and the actor nearly drowned in the process), dogs sniffed round the field of the dead after the Battle of Tewkesbury. It was a process that could easily go too far and eventually did so in a London street scene in *Richard III* full of horses and cattle and screaming chickens which was unanimously thrown out. The battle sequence had to be wholly convincing and it was here that all the television techniques of intercutting and montages of pre- shot sequences were invaluable and gave something that could never be conveyed in the theatre. It was here, too, that the hand-held camera came into its own, plunging through the smoke and the press of fighting men. It also turned out to have limitless possibilities as a subjective instrument. It became the walls of Coventry receiving the thrust of a battering-ram, and in the last desperate fight between Richard and Richmond the intrepid camerman would be- come at one moment Richard with a spiked ball and chain swinging across the front of the picture and at another Richmond cleaving his opponent with a sword.

The transfer is not always so complex. Another Royal Shakespeare Company production, Trevor Nunn's version of *Macbeth* (1976), was screened with notable simplicity and to great effect. The original production was staged in the RSC's second smaller theatre at Stratford-upon-Avon, The Other Place. It took full account of the facts that Shakespeare wrote the play for performance without scenery and for performance in what must have been a surprisingly intimate atmosphere with few members of the audience many feet away from the front of the thrust stage. Nunn's production took place on a bare floor with no scenery and with just a few props. When Thames Television recorded it, they allowed only a minimum of scenery to intrude between the viewer, actors and the text, relying extensively on close-ups and voice-overs (for soliloquies, sometimes intercut with action). It proved to be almost irresistible (if somewhat harrowing) viewing and should have been an object lesson to designers of future Shakespearean productions for television.

When mounting its own productions of Shakespeare, television has had varying degrees of success. Perhaps the most ambitious project so far has been 'The BBC Television Shakespeare', begun in 1979. All thirty-seven plays are included, being recorded over a six-year period. At times, it is a venture which looks as though it has been devised entirely for the export trade: Shakespeare as it is 'meant' to look. *Romeo and Juliet*, one of the earlier productions, was especially disappointing. A large and distracting set drew attention away from the words and made for little involvement. The design for *The Tempest* (see Chapter 7) was a much happier marriage of content and style. Under the production of Jonathan Miller, the third and fourth years of the project saw a much defter realisation of the plays then being tackled. Scenery was reduced to a 'vivid minimum' and Miller made Shakespeare on television into what it should be (according to his boss, Shaun Sutton): 'Fine actors delivering lines of genius in conditions of absolute clarity'. It should incidentally be noted that the BBC has not had a monopoly of Shakespeare. For example, in 1983, Granada Television mounted a much-praised production of *King Lear*, with Laurence Olivier as the king, and with direction by Michael Elliott. Interestingly its strengths were in the acting (and therefore presumably in thorough rehearsals) and not in televisual tricks.

Classic drama is not simply Shakespeare. Other playwrights have suffered an equal diversity of fates, especially in BBC Television's prestigious 'Play of the Month' slot. Occasionally these have had a distinct 'It's time we did a Strindberg' look about them. Often they are enthusiastic reworkings of very good plays. Most successful have been those which were true to the spirit of the original, where there had been judicious script-editing and where a young director was not trying to advance his reputation for creativity at the expense of solid craftsmanship.

The plays of the Restoration dramatists, of Congreve, Sheridan, Wilde and Shaw, of the great European and American playwrights and of modern 'classic' authors such as Rattigan, Pinter and Osborne can all triumph in the theatre. It would be silly for television drama departments to ignore them simply for that reason. Not only can such departments introduce new audiences to great plays they might otherwise never see, they can reinterpret and find new qualities within the classics. Because they are very good scripts, they present an exciting challenge to all the creative departments which work on television drama. Perhaps after all it is only the television dramatists who resent the position held by theatre plays so near the top of Hugh Whitemore's hierarchy of television drama.

Documentary Dramas

There are some very wise people in the television business of whom it is said that they can immediately tell the difference between drama documentaries, documentary drama, dramatic reconstructions, historical plays and factions. There may or may not be differences: here (for reasons to be given later) the one term, documentary dramas, will be used to embrace all the genuinely 'dramatic' manifestations of the genre.

In a *Radio Times* review of one such play, *Leeds – United!* by Colin Welland, Jonathan Raban sketched the television origins of the form:

The writer, director, and producer of a television play have the odds stacked against them. They have to make their slice of imaginary life look as real as the rest of that unending stream of screened events – the football matches, wars, riots, Miss World contests, government upheavals and show-jumping galas. *Play for Today* goes out after the *News*. But beside a Belfast bombing or Mr Healey, can a mere play ever seem anything but insipid, irrelevant and faked?

Nearly ten years ago now, the *Wednesday Play* team found a solution of sorts. Their plays made news because they were made *like* news. *Cathy Come Home* crudely spotlighted the plight of homeless mothers; *The Lump* drew the attention of the nation – and the Inland Revenue – to the army of self-employed casual labourers on building sites. By imitating TV journalism, the drama department stole some of the journalism's thunder.[11]

Cathy Come Home by Jeremy Sandford was first shown in 1966. In practice, it was not the first example of its kind by any means. A series of 'social dramas' by Colin Morris and Gilchrist Calder dating from the late fifties had been classified as 'documentaries', presumably because of their themes. They, like *Cathy Come Home, The Lump* and *Leeds – United!* were scripted plays, albeit ones using unknown actors and actual locations so as to portray 'reality' as closely as possible.

They were indisputably dramas, examples of fiction. They were introduced by the 'Play for Today' title sequence; they closed with a cast list. However, commentators on the media and subsequently the public began to worry about the dividing-line between reality and fiction. Are we watching the story of a real inebriate? Was that an actual pit accident? Was that a real policeman accepting a bribe? Because of this supposed uncertainty, but perhaps more because these plays were portraying unpalatable social truths, they were attacked precisely for being good fiction.

Some of the confusion might have been avoided (and might still be avoided) if we were to refer to them as 'documentary dramas', which classifies them firmly as (fictional) dramas, rather than the often-used 'drama documentaries', which implies they are documentaries. Whichever term is used, the genre consists of more than realistic social fictions. There have been fully dramatised biographies of historical figures, such as Charles Darwin, of characters from recent history, such as George VI or Winston Churchill, and of living people – for example, those involved in the Suez episode or eccentrics such as Quentin Crisp (sensitively played by John Hurt in Thames Television's play *The Naked Civil Servant*). Frequently these plays have used letters, diaries and speeches to incorporate the actual words spoken by real people. There have been further variations. *On Giant's Shoulders* was the story of a thalidomide child who appeared in 'his' play. Television reporters have appeared playing themselves reporting on fictional events.

Another variant has been the series of programmes devised by Granada Television's *World in Action* team. This news-magazine programme hit upon the idea of using journalists to improvise possible scenarios of actual events such as a cabinet meeting, using what material and 'inside information' was available. One particular one was roundly condemned by another journalist, Paul Johnson:

> It was shown to a mass audience, at peak-time, on the eve of the one event in the parliamentary calendar which impinges directly and deeply on the lives of all of us. It claimed to present the exact sequence of events and decisions which preceded the Budget, not in the form of speculation and guesswork, but in the shape of Ministers themselves, impersonated by journalists, mouthing the arguments they actually used in the secrecy of Number Ten. It was introduced with deadly seriousness, indeed with marked solemnity, at a time and under a title belonging to a straightforward current affairs programme. Yet it was nothing of the sort. It was a play, a work of fiction.[12]

He went on to generalise about the form:

> Actors are hired to impersonate real people, and professional playwrights to invent lines for them. The genre was first conceived as a means to 're-create' (that is, interpret) the

immediate past, and to 'portray' (that is, caricature) the
dead. More recently, it has been extended to embrace the
living and to deal not with historical events but current
ones. The object, quite brazenly, is to influence opinion on
contentious matters. The viewer does not know whether he
is getting theatre or documentary. In fact, he is getting a bit
of both, inextricably mixed.

Naturally, he is confused. That appears to be the object of
the game. Fiction supplies the gaps left in the authentic
documents, gaps which exist, as a rule, for the good and
sufficient reason that the events portrayed never happened
in real life. The producer of the television 'faction' does all in
his power to prevent the viewer distinguishing between the
two types of 'evidence' and to persuade him that all is
authentic. The introduction of genuine material makes the
programme more, not less, dishonest, for the mingling of
truth and fiction is of the very essence of propaganda.

Many others, in and out of parliament, echoed Paul Johnson's concern. Some took the trouble to draw a distinction
between what they called 'drama-documentaries' (realistic
plays about matters of social concern) and 'faction' (scripted
plays based on and incorporating actuality). To outlaw both
would of course deprive us of much fiction and biography.

Answering some of the criticism, Robin Sutch made the
same point:

Faction has actually been around for quite some time.
Aeschylus dramatised the recent Greek victory at
Marathon (490 BC) in *The Persians*. Shakespeare was the
first great faction writer in his history plays, and indeed
most Jacobean drama is based on what was considered
historical fact at the time. Webster's Dukes and Jim Jones
have several similarities, not least their potential for dramatic exploitation. 'Faction' is a neologism to describe what is
anything but a new phenomenon.[13]

He too went on to make a distinction between the varieties of
the genre:

Faction operates between the two poles of documentary and fictional drama. *Cathy Come Home* and similar programmes are nearest the documentary pole; in the middle are such programmes as *Churchill and the Generals* and *Edward and Mrs Simpson*, where all the characters are historical individuals. Nearer the fictional pole are programmes like *Holocaust*, with characters half historical and half fictional.

It is difficult to accept this analysis. *Holocaust* and *Cathy Come Home* have surely more in common with each other than either has with the 'historical' plays. What did, however, seem a particularly valid point in Sutch's article was the following: 'The debate should not centre on whether the genre is intrinsically good or bad, but on what constitutes good faction, what bad.'

Some of the problems that beset documentary dramas have been noted in reviews of the plays mentioned above. Jonathan Raban praised much of the realism of *Leeds – United!*, noting how its director, Roy Battersby, used the techniques of news cameramen when filming, for example, an 'interview' with a fictional trade-union secretary. As in a news programme, the official was seen talking past the camera to an unseen interviewer and was identified by a superimposed caption. However, Raban had a mixed response to Colin Welland's script:

He caught exactly the way that people speak in public; and the climactic set-piece in Leeds Town Hall was a triumph of realistic writing. But close-up, in private conversation, people suddenly turned, disconcertingly, into actors doing a script. A telephone call between two of the bosses was as creaky as anything in *The Brothers*. 'It's not our tin-pot rise they're singing for,' said one; 'it's their supper! They've a deep-rooted angry discontent that's been simmering for years. If that blows its top you'll never stop it!'

Those words might have sounded all right in a speech. Spoken into a telephone in an empty room, they were hopelessly phoney. The trouble is that once a TV play sets out to trick the viewer into mistaking it for documentary reality, it cannot afford to take these useful liberties with

life. *Leeds – United!* tried to have it both ways. It wanted
stage villains and melodrama; it also wanted to be as 'real'
as a *Tuesday's Documentary.*[14]

The problem of presenting 'villains' convincingly also be-
devilled *Holocaust*, Gerald Green's mammoth (seven-and-a-
quarter hours long) play about concentration-camp atrocities,
according to Joseph Hone's review in *The Listener*:

> The makers of *Holocaust* – seduced by the overwhelming
> moral right on their side – overscored everything that
> concerned the victims and never properly developed either
> the rationale of their persecutors or the divergent attitudes
> of some other Germans at the time. The whole seven-and-a-
> quarter hours passed in a strange historical vacuum of
> absolute black and white with no awkward greys in be-
> tween. In short, *Holocaust* was the ultimate in TV saints
> and sinners – which I do not suggest is untrue historically:
> simply that the clumsy narrative imbalance employed to
> present this truth made the whole thing seem *less* true than
> it should have been.[15]

One can sympathise with the writers and directors. Absolute realism would have been undramatic, even boring. Every-
day conversation is punctuated more by hesitation and repetition than by 'good lines'. No wonder a writer should be
tempted to script a strong confrontation. No wonder too that
the horrors of the concentration camp should provoke a writer
into using the deepest blacks to make his moral point. These,
however, are acceptable tricks of drama, not of documentaries. Their use is counter to the conventions of the latter and
it is by mixing conventions the documentary drama most often
fails.

The documentary-film maker avoids longueurs by filming
more than he needs, and then edits, selecting telling sentences
that illuminate the argument. He also allows each side to be
heard and (although he may structure his programme to give
one side more weight) it should ultimately be the viewer who
pronounces judgement.

Of course a documentary drama must to some extent tele-

scope events, be selective – but, if it is aiming at a documentary, historical realism, it must use the techniques of the
documentary whole-heartedly and not resort to invention. In
1981, Southern Television made a generally excellent
documentary serial, *Winston Churchill – The Wilderness
Years*. As David Wheeler pointed out, again in *The Listener*,

> For me the only really jarring moment came at the end of the
> first episode when Brendan Bracken, Churchill's protégé, is
> made to hurry to Chartwell with news of the offer of
> Dominion status to India – something Churchill must sure-
> ly have known about already. Otherwise, as a history
> lesson, it was hard to fault.[16]

The faults of *Leeds – United!*, *Holocaust* and *Winston
Churchill – The Wilderness Years* (as described above) strike
me as being artistic faults, where the makers of the plays have
embarked upon one style and then (perhaps because of lazi-
ness, perhaps because of a loss of nerve at not being 'dramatic'
enough) they have switched to another. Despite possible
artistic faults, they were 'realistic'. At the same time all were
demonstrably dramas and in no way 'dishonest', to use Paul
Johnson's term. They were not morally at fault.
    They did however have their own points of view and were to
some slight extent 'propaganda'. This though is the very
strength of modern drama (both in the theatre and on television): its discovery that it might hope to change opinion as
well as simply reflect it. To do this, it must have a factual
(documentary) base, as the playwright David Edgar has
observed of *Cathy Come Home*:

> The power of *Cathy Come Home* depended on the fact that
> its thesis – that British cities suffered from wretchedly
> inadequate housing at a time of presumed general prosperi-
> ty – was timely and true. Without that fact, *Cathy* would
> have been little more than a sad anecdote of an inadequate
> family destroyed by an indifferent bureaucracy. In reality,
> of course, the play changed the way we think about hous-
> ing. I think it changed the way we think about other things
> too – like the inner-city, the role of the social services, and

even the political system. Jeremy Sandford used his factual base in order to give dramatic force and credibility to a much wider theme.[17]

As we have seen, critics of the genre (such as Paul Johnson) complain particularly about this factual base. Interestingly, the attacks are rarely directed at plays and serials which use such a base to present an attractive (even glamorised) picture of, say, recent monarchs. More often the criticism is directed at plays such as *Churchill and the Generals* and *Suez 1956*. Both of these plays by Ian Curteis had a personal 'vision' about their central characters, Churchill and Eden. They were one man's visions, presented persuasively, by means of a documentary style, *within a drama*. Curteis is apparently insistent that all his works be labelled clearly as plays. There can be surely no objection to them in a free society where others are free to make their own deductions from known facts, or indicate where his plays are unrealistic or factually incorrect. If they convince and no such errors can be found, then perhaps they represent a truth (like *Cathy Come Home*).

Critics are right to condemn news and current-affairs pro-grammes when they employ actors to reconstruct scenes 'as they might have happened' and do not label them as 'recon-structions' or 'simulations'. The same critics have every right to condemn dramas which purport to be actuality, but so long as there is a writer's credit and a cast list clearly attached to the play then surely it is presumptuous to assume the public does not know what it is watching.

To repeat the quotation from Robin Sutch's article, the debate should concentrate 'on what constitutes good faction, what bad'. The best and most effective documentary dramas must be those with the strongest factual base.

Series and Serials

Television has its own way of marking the passing seasons of the year. Come September, come January, the programme journals are covered by a whole rash of little flags each announcing a 'New Series'. There are sound commercial reasons for this. Popular and 'accessible' weekly serial drama is one of the most effective ways of ensuring an audience stays loyal to a particular channel throughout one of the thirteen-week quarters into which television tends to divide the year. Indeed, it has been argued at some length by John Ellis[18] that the drama series (or serial) is television's most distinctive form: a 'segmental' narrative that viewers can stay with, episode by episode, yet at the same time not feel disorientated should they miss the occasional one. It must be of some satisfaction and relief to network controllers (and perhaps more to heads of drama) that the public continues to demonstrate an apparently insatiable appetite for such series and serials.

Once there was a clear division between the two forms. A series was what the term implies: a series of separate plays (by one or more writers) about a recurring group of characters, a constant location or an institution. The early crime series provided the most obvious examples of this genre. Each week, the leading detective would be involved in a different case, which would be unravelled and solved by the end of the play. Next week saw the start of a new case. In contrast, a serial involved a continuing story, each episode often ending with a 'cliff-hanger'. A series might be of as few as three episodes or as many as the inevitable thirteen (thus filling a 'season' of the television year). The term has also been applied to the unending series more often known as 'soaps' (q. v.).

During the 1970s, the divide between the two forms became less distinct. Possibly this was the result of a compromise between two conflicting desires. On the one hand, producers and planners welcomed the power of a serial to build up a loyal audience that would watch each episode (a fact particularly attractive to potential advertisers). On the other hand, there was the fear that a viewer who missed one episode might then give up the serial under the impression that he or she would not be able to catch up with the storyline. There were also objections to the series format from writers who resented the need to 'go back to the beginning' at the start of each episode. One of the weaknesses of the 'pure' series is that the hero must solve his problem (be it a crime or whatever) every week and in fifty minutes. In order to develop the naturalism that viewers now expect, some situations need longer to reach a climax and resolution. There must also be space and time to build up a complete character with weaknesses as well as strengths.

Whatever the reason for a compromise between the two genres, it resulted in series/serials such as *Secret Army*. Set in occupied Belgium in the Second World War, it told a story about the resistance movement. It was centred in a Brussels café which was both a headquarters of the movement and a favourite resort of Nazi officers. On one level, each episode was a self-contained story about, for example, a particular escaping British airman or an exercise in sabotage. On another level there would be a continuing story line about, perhaps, a love affair between two regular characters. There was also the underlying story of the progress of the war, a story which surfaced in the later episodes, when *Secret Army* became much more like a genuine serial than it had been in its early days; when, although only a very few of even those early episodes could have been shown out of sequence and not run into continuity problems, the viewer who missed one week's programme would still feel involved and informed a fortnight later.

There have been a number of other variations on the traditional forms. For example, there has been Yorkshire Television's series *Number 10*, a series about the private lives of seven prime ministers, set in Downing Street. In practice they were first shown out of chronological sequence and there were no recurring characters. All they had in common was a theme and the set, which was described in an IBA yearbook:

Perhaps the most outstanding technical feature of the series is the huge set, which was constructed in a massive old underground aircraft hangar alongside the Leeds and Bradford Airport in Yorkshire. The largest set ever built for a programme by Yorkshire Television, it is a near perfect reconstruction of Downing Street and the home of the First Lord of the Treasury, the official title of the Prime Minister. *Number 10*, produced by Margaret Bottomley, tells of the private lives of seven Prime Ministers as they were lived behind what is probably the best-known front door in the world. The subjects range in period from the 1700s –

William Pitt the Younger – to Ramsay MacDonald's first
period of office in the 1920s.

It was that time scale which caused some headaches for
the production team, for Downing Street's make-up has
changed considerably over the past 150 years. For example,
at one time there were two pubs in the street which, when it
was given to Robert Walpole by the then King, was the
centre of a rather poor, rough area. Over the years, build-
ings have been knocked down or changed as Downing
Street developed into the street we know today.

The staff at Number 10 itself could not have been more
helpful. Margaret Bottomley, the author Terence Feely, and
the designer Roger Andrews were given a conducted tour of
the building and considerable help with historical facts. A
huge publication called *A Survey of London* also proved
invaluable, and the Department of the Environment sup-
plied numerous photographs and prints. The interior sets of
Number 10, reconstructed in Yorkshire's own studios, were
not quite such a problem. The Board of Works have im-
maculate records of all work done inside the building, the
exact cost of every item, and even the colour with which
each room was decorated. Of course, certain pieces of
well-known furniture – the porter's chair in the hall for
example – had to be specially reproduced.[19]

Despite such loving attention to detail, the series did not
please every critic:

> For the opener we got Denis Quilley doing Gladstone in a
> balding wig and the late Celia Johnson working wondrously
> as his elfin, irresistible wife. Clearly we are not meant to
> learn much about the politics of the day – Terence Feely's
> script was full of things like 'What are we going to do about
> the Irish?' and 'The Russians are getting up to mischief in
> Afghanistan again.'
>
> No, what *Number 10* is about is The Private Lives of the
> Great, which in Mr Gladstone's case meant his nocturnal
> ramblings among the ladies of the kerbside. Did he or didn't
> he? Was he or wasn't he? It all started out like a wonderful
> animated penny dreadful, helped along no end by Herbert

Wise's compulsion to shoot Gladstone with Ripperesque eyebrows and a manic grin.[20]

Number 10 was a demonstration of the fact that you need more than a good idea and a bit of research to make a series. You need characters that are credible and that have a least some depth. A format alone is not enough.

Some of course would say that *Number 10* was neither a series nor a serial but an 'anthology', a term sometimes applied to a group of separate plays linked together by a theme and a title. Granada Television has used this device to give a 'brand image' to what were actually six single plays about personal relationships. *All for Love*, based on different short stories, was packaged to have the appearance of a short series, which presumably was to build viewer loyalty and to attract advertisers who might have been frightened by a run of disparate single plays. Other examples have been Channel 4's occasional series 'First Love', which has included loves as varied as teenage crushes and a groundsman's passion for his cricket pitch, and Central's quartet of film dramas *Birth of a Nation*. While the former series was by different writers, *Birth of a Nation* and another equally uncompromising 'anthology' of plays, *Boys from the Blackstuff*, were each by just one author. The *Boys from the Blackstuff* also had the same set of recurring characters.

The 'boys' had appeared originally in a single play, *The Black Stuff*, when, as a tarmac-laying gang, they were to a certain extent working in Middlesbrough. In the series, they were back on their home patch of Liverpool, out of work and wrestling with the Department of Health and Social Security. The opening episode had them moonlighting for a shady builder who was ironically trying to complete a contract on a new employment exchange. In subsequent episodes one character, Yosser, breaks under the pressure of unemployment and its related problems; in another, one of his mates, Dixie Dean, is dragged into the criminal underworld. In other plays, two other recurring characters, Chrissie and Loggo, are tempted into fraud and caught, and a further character, George, meets his death. Critics analysed its subtleties and symbolism; its black comedy, despair and gloom. In any period, it deserved its rave reception, but some of its success must have been owing to the fact that it was a series of plays which found its time and struck an emotional chord not just on Merseyside, an area Bleasdale feels so strongly for, but in the West Midlands, the North East and even in protected London. It showed too how a format can embrace and convey important ideas and social conviction.

Its author, Alan Bleasdale, claims to be equally hostile to both the political Left and Right. He is more concerned with victims. Nevertheless it is a political series, and one that helped viewers to identify with contemporary issues. It was in a Liverpool pub that one viewer met Alan Bleasdale. 'I like your series. Great. 'Cept that every time I see it, I want to hang myself.'

It was therefore the sort of series that is championed by those who feel that the central responsibility of television drama is 'to engage with the social and political problems of contemporary Britain' (to quote one speaker at the 1983 Edinburgh Television Festival). Those who hold such views feel that popular television series (or serials) must take on some of the obligations and convictions maintained by the single play in earlier decades. To them, costume drama is simply escapist.

Given the lack of slots for serious drama, one can appreciate that viewpoint. Set against it must be the continuing demand for popular drama and some gratitude that drama of any sort should be seen as such a necessary component of the schedules. Moreover, there are signs that popular taste is becoming more discerning and that a series with weak plots or superficial characterisation is unlikely to hold its audience. Many important lessons were learned from what was generally accepted to be a disastrous failure, BBC Television's *The Borgias*. Abysmal (and often incomprehensible) dialogue and tortuous plots were not redeemed by elaborate costume or even a revealing lack of it. As John Naughton commented in *The Listener*,

> To those who made the series, *The Borgias* must have seemed to have everything: sex, violence, gluttony, the Vatican, the murderous intrigues of that famous

Spanish–Italian family. Actually the first episode had all these, and lacked only English subtitles to clarify the unintelligible dialogue, and a set of dense historical footnotes to explain the political and familial issues embroiled in the saga. The overall impression, I'm afraid, was not promising – it smacked of fanciful absurdity, with a cast of overdressed ciphers struggling to establish themselves as stereotypes, led by Adolfo Celi as a Rodrigo who was beautiful to look at, but whose Eengleesh ees no furry goot.[21]

Costume drama was shown to need the highest dramatic qualities as well as historical accuracy in order to please a discerning audience.

Similarly it would once have been hard to imagine that a deliberately light-hearted look at the shady world of backstreet deals would need to have such rich characterisation and quite such a subtle mixture of comedy, action and realism as Thames Television's *Minder*, or as had the BBC's *Shoestring* or *Bergerac*. These last two are good examples of how the detective series has matured from the days when PC Dixon plodded his way round Dock Green.

Drama series may not have the prestige of the single play, the writer may resent the format, and the actor may worry about being typecast. The series may not receive the critical acclaim accorded to the screening of a major theatre play or even to a documentary drama, but there is no doubt that the range of the series and the serial as made in Britain is remarkable. Writers have proved that it is possible to say something of importance within a format and actors have shown that subtleties of interpretation will be appreciated. In return the viewers have demonstrated they will be at first selective but, once pleased, will continue to watch in their millions.

The Classic Serial and Adaptations

For over thirty years, a significant and generally prestigious component of the drama output has been the serial dramatisation of 'classic' novels, and (more recently) of modern novels. Jane Austen, the Brontës, Trollope, and especially Dickens have all been served up in thirty- or fifty-minute episodes with varying degrees of success. Dickens in particular has transferred effectively to this form, perhaps because his novels were originally published in serial form in magazines.

One climax was reached in the serialisation of the novels of John Galsworthy which form *The Forsyte Saga*. This epic serial captured the public imagination just before colour television gave a new impetus to an already thriving genre. Not all serials have been so successful, perhaps because 'a blanket of Victoriana' has smothered a production, resulting in something that was visually enticing yet devoid of the intellectual sharpness of the novel that was its begetter. Alternatively, financial and artistic caution have descended like a fog, restricting invention and ambition. As the one-time BBC head of serials, Shaun Sutton, has recorded,

> Television cannot always match the huge sweep of the great classics. *War and Peace* sends armies marching across its pages; television must be content with regiments, even companies. The TV screen is small, and its domestic picture often far from perfect. Television drama is a foreground matter, with actors communicating close to a very personal audience. But there is a point where sparse economy must be discouraged. The television viewer has been visually spoiled by the extravagancies of old feature films, with their vast crowds and gigantic settings. The streets of a television Dickensian London must not look as empty as if there had been some terrible disaster, and it is no longer enough to represent the Battle of Waterloo by three dead soldiers, one riderless horse, and a Crimean War cannon. An artistic course must be laid between prudence and parsimony.[22]

This trend towards a more ambitious style was noted in *The Listener* in early 1983:

> It used to be that television was interested in culling a kind of cultural respectability from 'classic' literature. More recently though, with the growth of a global market for

television programmes, both the BBC and the ITV companies have discovered that period adaptations are among their biggest export earners. Prestige adaptations like Granada's *Brideshead Revisited* now attract huge amounts of 'co-production' finance. And the productions that result increasingly share the same kind of 'look' or style: sumptuous, high-gloss period detail allied to languidly paced, cinematic framing.[23]

The new style reached a high-water mark with the abovementioned *Brideshead Revisited*. To quote again from *The Listener*,

> *Brideshead Revisited* (Granada), a visual orgy, has already driven Fleet Street demented from trying to calculate its cost. By the time I got to the press preview, the estimates were larger than the annual budget of the BBC, a sum which induced one elegant lady journalist to berate the PR staff for their failure to finish the job properly by providing free champagne for the assembled hacks. Actually, there was no need for bubbly, for the first episode promised intoxication in abundance, and in so doing faithfully reflected the tone of the novel itself.[24]

A glamorous, exotic or aristocratic background has often contributed in no small way to the success of a serial adaptation. Besides the affluence of the Forsytes and the grandeur of Brideshead, there has been the genteel dignity of the country houses in *Pride and Prejudice* and of the Close at Barchester. A sense of entering 'another world' has been a keynote of other serials, even when they have been set in the present and in mundane locations. John le Carré's two spy novels *Tinker, Tailor, Soldier, Spy* and *Smiley's People* involved scenes in London streets, on Primrose Hill and in less attractive parts of Europe; yet to some critics, these serials were confusing and pretentious. One reason may have been le Carré's method of allowing his characters to tell the plot through dialogue. This makes for a particularly smooth and accurate translation from novel to television, but it does mean that the viewer must also be an attentive listener. The plot and the mystery are resolved as much through conversations as by means of car chases. Another reason may have been that le Carré is in fact writing serious novels about human values which happen almost incidentally to be spy stories. Many who dismissed the television serials were perhaps hoping for straightforward thrillers without a subtext which explored such themes as loyalty, marriage and the English class system. Luckily the series also had their champions, who pointed out just how the writing, acting, direction, camerawork and post-production skills combined to create something that was both a work of art and intelligent and entertaining television. They were directed by Simon Langton.

The BBC, as producer of such serials, has achieved much praise for its adaptations. There have been dissident voices, notably (and perhaps surprisingly considering his own involvement in the BBC Television Shakespeare) Jonathan Miller. At the 1983 Edinburgh Television Festival, he attacked the BBC's tendency 'to preen itself on the transformation of the novel into a dramatised serial'. He went on to insist that 'novels are an absolutely untranslatable art form and do not prosper on television, except in the case of the trivial or second-rate novel, when it doesn't matter what happens to them anyway'. Speeches made (as that one was) at a time when the speaker is changing career often have the primary purpose of convincing the speaker that he or she is making the correct career choice. Nevertheless, Dr Miller was right to point out that novels are 'untranslatable'. What appears on screen is not the experience of the novel but a television serial made out of the novel. Despite the doctor, many novels have prospered as television serials and have gained new popularity because of their adaptation. As television drama they may lack originality. They may pander to the schedulers who think the public will like a serial with a recognised title. Yet who would have predicted that a tale of decadent, aristocratic lapsed Catholics would have proved as popular as did *Brideshead Revisited*? Dr Miller may of course classify Waugh's novel as trivial or second-rate. It certainly prospered in its television form and both before that and subsequently as a novel.

Television does plunder in its search for material. Some

novels have suffered badly in its greedy hands. All must be compressed, edited, even filleted in order to be fitted into a preordained number of episodes, each of the same duration. The fact that the adaptation is sometimes clumsy should not damn the process. The classic serial or serial adaptation is not planned to be 'original drama' not is it intended to be a reproduction of the novel. Of course it has a loyalty to its inspiration but it should be judged for being itself, another and distinctive form of television drama.

Soap Opera

It is a convention that any discussion of soap opera (or 'soaps' to use a subtly even more disparaging term) should begin with the disclaimer that it is an American invention and British television is not to blame. Certainly it originated in the States, in fact as an advertising-vehicle on commercial radio, where daily serials existed to promote the products of particular manufacturers, notably those of the detergent makers Proctor and Gamble; hence the name. The form was taken up by television on both sides of the Atlantic, and if Britain was not the original perpetrator then that is not to suggest that it has not become a staple part of television drama in this country.

Although it is the intention of this book to concentrate on British television practice, it is in this case illuminating to digress in order to note the production process involved in an American daily soap opera, as described by Peter Fiddick:

> American soap-opera factories are production lines such as to make General Motors look like a craftsman coach-builder. The name of the game being addiction, a bid to capture the consumer-spending female audience for a network's advertisers, true soapers are strictly afternoon fare, the mornings being packed with hyper-active game shows. They appear at the same time, on the same channel, not weekly, or in bursts but 'stripped', in the jargon, across every single day of every week. From soon after noon until 4 p.m. all three main commercial networks grind them out, end to end.

At the studios, the cast come in every morning, read through, get as much direction as they and the cameras can take in the time, tape the show – and stagger home with the next day's script to learn. Little wonder that soap-opera proper is a thing of cardboard sets, cardboard scripts, fluffed cues and static discussion of off-stage events.[25]

Britain has not yet produced a daily serial, *Crossroads* approaching closest to that frequency with four episodes a week until 1980, when the Independent Broadcasting Authority intervened and decreed that it would become only thrice-weekly. Most other British manifestations of the form have been twice-weekly or even only weekly. Some, such as *Crossroads*, do not 'rest' but continue throughout the year. Others, such as *Emmerdale Farm*, are rested for seasons and then return. The mark of them all is that they are continuing serials, usually with a strong central location permitting an endless variety of stories as the established characters gossip, work, love and quarrel together and behind each other's backs.

From its early days, soap opera has achieved an amazing response from viewers who identify closely with their ersatz television 'neighbours'. Viewers send flowers to characters on their weddings and wreaths to fictional funerals, while applications are received by the producing companies from families apparently seriously keen to move into an empty house on an imaginary street.

Critics sneer at the fantasy dressed up as reality, at the glib and easy solutions offered to serious social problems and at simplistic storylines. However, sociologists and programme makers both point out the reassurances the serials offer to their viewers, to their maintenance of traditional values and their ability to promote good causes. Whatever assessment is favoured, soap operas remain intensely popular with viewers – as is shown by the ratings. At the time of writing the latest monthly figures available were those for August 1983. In the 'top fifty' (that is, the programmes with most viewers that month), the top eight places were taken by the eight editions of *Coronation Street*. *Crossroads* took seven of the remaining places in the top twenty.

Mention of *Coronation Street* brings us to another of the conventions of discussions about soap operas. In any such discussion, time and space must be found to consider whether *Coronation Street* is indeed an example of the genre or whether it is the great classic serial of all time. Whenever it is mentioned in the same paragraph as obvious 'soaps', executives of Granada Television (its makers) are supposed to leap up in order to announce that it is a 'proper' drama serial which only happens to be shown twice weekly. 'Why,' they say, 'even Sir John Betjeman and Lord Olivier like it.' In all honesty, it does fit almost any definition of a soap opera, except that it is of vastly superior quality compared to most of its rivals. Its writing, acting and direction are stylish by any television drama standards. Its plots and story-lining demonstrate an assured confidence and a skill born of the ability to learn from the mistakes of others. It is also frequently very funny. Even though readers of books such as this are meant to uphold the superiority of the single play, it might be safe for them to approve of *Coronation Street*. It is after all often better constructed than many a single play.

Despite the virtues of *Coronation Street*, the soap operas are often mocked and often deservedly so. In many the dialogue is artificial and clumsy, the direction is banal, the acting indifferent (and often under-rehearsed) and the production penny-pinching. No wonder they attract criticism, but such attacks are not always dispassionate, as Peter Buckman noted in a *Listener* article 'in praise of soaps':

> Behind this [criticism] is a sneer at people who are hooked on what appears to be the same people doing the same things week after week. But no amount of reviewers' criticism will alter the economy of producing soap operas, which by its very nature has to be cheap and fast (and which, of course, is very profitable). And to pick on its imperfections is to miss the function of the genre, which is to tease, from a complicated weave of plots, a number of endings that will reassure the audience, reinforce their beliefs (you won't hear of a revolutionary soap any more than you will of a radical fairytale), and above all keep them tuned.[26]

To a large extent, it is the careful interweaving of stories that achieves that last aim. Each episode needs to end with one or more storylines at some sort of 'cliff-hanging' stage to tempt viewers to return to the serial. Consequently, as any one story reaches a stage of resolution, another must be started. Planners need to take a huge number of other factors into account in order to bring about the situation in which the viewer will theoretically never stop watching, because there is always some situation she (or less frequently, he) wants to see resolved. Obviously the planners will not want to 'use up' a character or group of characters by allowing them to feature too frequently as the focus of a story. They must also be aware of more mundane factors, such as leaving time for actors to go on holiday. Additionally they must ensure the leading actors gain enough work from their commitment to the serial. (Some will be paid by the appearance rather than being salaried, or be on substantial retainers.)

Other devices are used to encourage viewers to stay loyal to a particular serial. First, it should always be possible for a viewer to miss an episode and not feel out of touch. (Hence the reaction of some irregular viewers who feel that, no matter how long they stay away from a serial, nothing seems to have happened in the interim. The cynic would say it is a mark of soap operas that an event happens every fifth episode and the characters talk about it for the intervening ones.) Secondly, and paradoxically, the regular viewer should feel more deeply involved the more he or she watches. For example, the regular viewer of *Coronation Street* will place any minor setback that happens to Ken Barlow in the context of the many setbacks this character has suffered over the years. An aside by the barmaid, Bet Lynch, may be all the more piquant to the initiate who knows she has had an illegitimate child. In this way, a soap opera can build upon the viewer's interest in gossip and delight at 'being in the know'. Thirdly, a soap opera can, indeed must, please its regular viewers by ensuring that its principals behave in character: 'Above all, the soaps are the property of their fans. That public outcry did not stop Meg Mortimer's departure does not alter the fact that no other drama is so influenced by what its viewers think.'[27]

Given the fact that the viewers of soap operas are mainly women, this is perhaps why so many of them are dominated by strong female characters. For years the above-mentioned Meg Mortimer (previously Meg Richardson) was the dominant character in *Crossroads*. Perhaps to emphasise her position of power, her second husband was frequently away on business trips. Before that she had been straightforwardly 'a widow'. Another widow, Annie Sugden, dominates *Emmerdale Farm*, and *Coronation Street* has been the territory of a series of dominating females from Ena Sharples to Annie Walker and Elsie Tanner. Male characters may occasionally be mature, even sexually available. More frequently they are rogues, idlers or simply inadequate.

One of the artistic attractions of the continuing soap opera is the space it offers its writers. To quote Peter Buckman again,

> The soap writer can develop a character over years at almost the pace of life itself. For example, *Crossroads'* fans will have watched simple-minded Benny progress from incompetence to a touching, if limited, ability over the years: no playwright could make a national hero out of such unpromising material within the confines of a single play.

It is noteworthy that, despite the BBC's early involvement in the genre with such serials as *The Grove Family* (including its devastating caricature of a grandma) and *Compact* (set in the editorial offices of a woman's magazine), it has been left to the ITV companies to produce the main soap operas over the last fifteen years or so. True, there have been the BBC's weekly 'glossy' soaps such as *The Brothers* (where, typically, the long-distance haulage firm was a matriarchy) and (on a much superior level) *When the Boat Comes In*. However, it has been left to ATV (and subsequently Central Television) with *Crossroads*, Granada with *Coronation Street* and Yorkshire Television with *Emmerdale Farm* to act as the main providers. There have been others. For example, Southern Television produced *Together*, set in a housing-association block of flats, and Scottish Television screened *Take the High Road*, a strange mixture of travelogue and social comment.

More interestingly there has been *Brookside*, produced by an independent company for Channel 4. Set in a Merseyside private housing-estate, it proved a cornerstone of that network's viewing-figures and broke new ground in production techniques. It is discussed more fully in Chapter 8.

The role of the independent producer may develop further. Another such company, Limehouse Productions, has expressed a commitment to produce a twice-weekly soap for cable television. At the same time there are signs of further investment by the traditional providers. In late 1983, Granada Television was rumoured to be piloting four possible soaps, including ones set in a group medical practice, the London gambling-world, a group of army wives and the Cheshire middle classes (all tightly knit communities typical of those featured in soap operas). At the same time, the BBC bought the former ATV studios at Elstree partly with the intention of using them for the production of a new major soap opera.

The purpose of soap operas is to be popular. They build audiences for advertisers and for particular channels. The serious drama critic may properly be highly critical of their standards. Despite some notable exceptions (often within the much-maligned *Crossroads*, which has, for example, included story lines aimed at countering racial discrimination and heightening awareness of the needs of the disabled), they exist to pander to popular prejudice rather than to educate public opinion. They may be very close to the bottom of Hugh Whitemore's hierarchy (see pp. 1–2), but they have helped to cement an expectation for drama within the television schedules. As Peter Buckman concluded in his *Listener* article, 'There is no need to treat the soaps with undue seriousness – but it is time for them to receive the respect to which their following and achievements entitle them.'

We turn now to the three media by which television drama may be presented. Many plays include a mixture: for example, a play recorded mainly on video tape in a studio may also include previously *filmed* scenes made on location. For the sake of clarity in this introductory chapter, the media will be considered separately.

Live Television

In the early days of television, all drama was of course 'live'; that is, performed in the studio at the time of transmission.

Pre-recording on video tape became usual in the 1960s, but even as late as 1975 there was a regular live drama series, *The Eleventh Hour*, made by the BBC. It is easy now to forget that such significant series as *Z-Cars* were largely live (although they included filmed inserts).

Live television places all sorts of strains and restrictions on those involved in its creation and in no form of live television more than in drama. Actors tell terrible stories of appearing in live dramas at Alexandra Palace, particularly when two studios were being used in the same production: of having to race along a corridor in full armour after one exit in time for an entrance a few seconds later 'in another part of the forest'. Not only actors but also cameramen needed to be strong and fleet of foot, as heavy pedestal cameras had to be trundled from scene to scene. Typically, a television play might have involved four or five scenes or 'sets' arranged around the studio, with the cameras on an island in the centre, able to look into each set in turn. The tale is regularly told, with relish and suitable embellishments, of the novice director who failed to plot his camera moves thoroughly in advance. As his play progressed, the cameras circled each other continuously until, with the play only half completed, they were knotted firmly together by their cables, incapable of any further movement.

Normally, little went wrong. Perhaps an actor would fluff a line, perhaps a microphone boom came accidentally into shot. But to achieve such excellence meant many hours of rehearsal. Unlike present practice, in which theatrical rehearsal (of the actors by the director) is followed by technical realisation, technicians would have to spend several days rehearsing with the cast, to perfect complicated movements of cameras with their sprawling cables, of microphones and even lights.

Live drama consequently placed restrictions on the writers, as directors sometimes had to point out. 'I know it would be nice, love, but Camera 3 is up the other end of the studio.' 'Yes dear, super contrast, but she'll never change from riding-kit into full evening-dress in ten seconds.' A script had to be 'possible'. Once a performance started, there was no way of pausing (as there is when working on to tape) to sort out a technical crisis or retake a crucial scene.

Another feature of drama before the days of easy taping was the fact that a scheduled repeat meant the whole cast and crew reassembling for the second performance. Thus, in 1954, when the BBC's production of a dramatisation of George Orwell's *1984* caused a national furore (because of the horrific scenes involving torture, rats, and the novel's generally depressing view of the future), there was a debate not about the planned 'repeat' but about 'the second performance'. The four-day gap between the two performances, with every daily paper pontificating on the play, must have been strange ones for Michael Barry, then head of BBC Television Drama, and for the cast.

Interestingly, BBC Television experimented once again with live drama in early 1983. Five plays were transmitted 'as they happened' from the Pebble Mill studios at Birmingham. Once again those working on them found the need for a much longer period of collaboration between cast and crew. All the tricks of 'post-production' (the adding of sound effects, music, titles, and so forth) had to be worked out in detail in advance and incorporated into the studio process. Such of course was the practice before recording. The professed aim of the Pebble Mill experiment was not simply 'nostalgia', but a desire to find a new style of drama which broke some of the naturalistic conventions which have become associated with television drama. For example, the opening play, *The Battle of Waterloo* by Keith Dewhurst, told its story with only sixteen actors, no extras and no set. The result was something so different from most television drama that critics and viewers were uncertain how to judge it. Technically it was a considerable success, although the numerous rehearsals held to iron out all possible problems meant that it was not quite as spontaneous as it might have been. It certainly prompted the thought that, if God had meant us to do live drama, He would never have given us video tape.

Film

But, before there was video tape, there was film. Indeed, film was the first recording-medium used in television. Actually, some people have been inclined to think of film as the medium of cinema movies and not of television. Certainly in the early years of television, when the two industries looked on each other with some hostility, there was little interchange of working-methods.

Until 1951, American television drama was performed live (as was British practice). In that year, in America, Lucille Ball had her new situation comedy, *I Love Lucy*, shot in a studio as usual but not with live television cameras. Instead it was filmed on three 35 mm film cameras. The experiment was highly successful and soon the use of film spread to many television series, such as the first television police shows and Westerns, where the fluidity and pace of film gave added excitement.

In Britain, television developed differently. The BBC and the ITV companies had invested heavily in studio facilities. Such investment had to be utilised to the full and that meant that film became a luxury – hence the idea that it was to be used in television drama only for scenes which could not be staged in a studio (an idea strongly supported by cost-conscious accountants).

Normally 16 mm film is used, of one of two different types. Ektachrome is the cheaper and easier to use, because only one developing-process is required and it produces an image which can be broadcast directly. For this reason it is often used in news programmes. It has the disadvantage of scratching easily. The other type is called Eastman Color, which produces a negative image from which a 'cutting' print is made. Its colour qualities are generally thought to be more natural and more subtle.

In practice, the basic way of filming is to use one camera with a microphone linked to a high-quality tape recorder. For each shot, the camera is moved to its new position. Consequently filming is a slow, lengthy business, often with much waiting around (if the filming is out of doors) waiting for low-flying aircraft to disappear from skies that supposedly stretch above a Victorian mansion or for the sun to regain the brilliance it was exhibiting in the previous shot. There are many attractions to film-making, however. The equipment is comparatively light and mobile. There are no cumbersome cables trailing from camera to recording-van. The director can stand close by the camera, in immediate contact with actors and cameraman. It is also very easy to edit the developed film. The film editor can make precise cuts, he does not have to make split-second decisions, he can even go back to the beginning and reassemble the shots in another sequence. Film-editing is an art form in its own right. As more than one director has said, 'A great film is made in the cutting-room.' Much as the purists and artists may praise the qualities and flexibility of film, it remains expensive. A day's work may result in about thirty minutes' worth of film being shot, out of which three minutes will be usable in the final production. There are other drawbacks. You cannot see the results of your day's work until later. More than one day's filming has been wasted when it has been discovered that there was a hair in the camera gate or that the film stock was faulty. However its enthusiasts (such as David Hare) remain convinced of its virtues:

> Every artist worth anything in the twentieth century has longed to work in it because it is quick and supple. It has wit. Film passes effortlessly from style to style. By angling, by heightening, by the slightest visual distortion your view of your material may alter in the passage of a single shot. Film is fast. It cuts well. You create your work like a mosaic out of tiny pieces, each one minutely examined as it's prepared, and then slipped into the stream of images you are preparing in your head.[28]

As we have said, British writers and directors have had to plead for every second's film that might be used to extend and illuminate a basically studio-bound play. Rare indeed was the budget that allowed a television play to be made entirely on location and on film. In recent years, however, the situation has been changing. Quite a sizeable amount of recent television drama has been made entirely on film. Many 'plays' could equally well have been labelled 'films', and one new slot on Channel 4 has been titled 'Film on Four'. It seems to mark the belated fusing of the two industries in this country (thirty years later than in America) to the mutual advantage of both.

Video Tape

Since the late fifties, it has been possible to record material coming from television cameras on to magnetic (or video) tape. It is like ordinary sound-recording tape and unlike film: when you hold it up you cannot see anything on it. The sound and pictures are recorded on it as a series of electro-magnetic pulses. To find out what is on it, it must be replayed on a video-tape recorder. This is its first and most obvious advantage. It can be rewound and replayed immediately after recording. There is no developing or printing-process.

When video-recording, several cameras can be used at once, each looking at the same scene from a different angle. A person called the vision mixer (under instructions from the director) selects which camera's output goes on to the tape.

At the moment, in Britain, various kinds of tape are in use. Some machines use 50 mm (two-inch) tape, some 25 mm (one-inch) tape and some 20 mm (three-quarter-inch) tape. Many engineers say that, the wider the tape, the better quality will be the pictures and sound.

The development of video tape meant that sections of live current affairs programmes could be pre-recorded. In drama it meant that whole plays could be recorded. No longer did studio drama have to be live. A play could be recorded in as many sections as proved necessary, and then edited together before transmission. Because several cameras are involved, longish sequences (even whole scenes) can be recorded without a break (unlike the situation when filming). Greater productivity is therefore possible when working with tape, compared with film. It is now generally expected within the BBC that a day's work in the studio should result in twenty to thirty minutes' drama being recorded.

For this reason, because there are no processing costs, and because tapes can even be 'wiped' and used again, video-recording is comparatively cheap. (Tragically, some priceless plays have been lost for posterity simply because managements have insisted on the reuse of tape.) Because of its cheapness, because of the facility of immediate replay (to check the quality of a performance, the technical quality or simply to check continuity) and because tape is less demanding than film so far as lighting is concerned, video-recording has its attractions.

That last point brings us to the use of video on location, to record either inserts for a studio play or a complete play. In the early days, a large outside-broadcast unit was a cumbersome affair. Four large cameras, miles of cable and huge vans to contain all the technical equipment did not make for excessive mobility. The necessarily large crew was a less friendly, less intimate group than its film counterpart. But video was speedier than filming and there was the argument that tape recorded on location matched studio scenes better than did film.

In recent years lightweight cameras, even hand-held ones, have increased mobility. Single-camera recording is being introduced and other filmic ways of working are being adopted. Slowly the differences are disappearing. Additionally, what has been another major criticism of video is also becoming invalid. Once, tape-editing was a clumsy process, with the tape itself having to be cut and spliced to gain the required sequences. Now it is edited electronically and to increasingly sophisticated effect. Perhaps the only remaining objection to tape is really an objection to studio work with the ever-present anxiety of over-running the allocated time and incurring expensive overtime payments and interfering with the next production due into that studio, right under the eagle eye of higher management. Away from the studio, director and producer are kings. In the building, there is always an executive on the sixth floor who can, at the flick of a switch, see exactly what is or is not being recorded in any studio.

For whatever reasons, studio (video) drama has its critics. At the 1983 Television Festival in Edinburgh, a famous producer and director, Richard Eyre, reviled what he described as the cost-cutting drive to make drama in the studio. 'The mechanics of the studio floor are an obstacle race . . . the studio play now looks as real as the country house drama.' He went on to describe film as the natural language of the century but admitted that one-camera location video work was acceptable. For Eyre, the studio play was a 'dead art'. Just how much television drama we should be able to afford without studio production is an open question.

2.
The Providers

BBC

The BBC is a 'body corporate', set up by Royal Charter and operating under licence. Its governors are appointed by the Crown or 'Queen in Council'. The original body was the British Broadcasting Company, which became the British Broadcasting Corporation on 1 January 1927.

Its domestic services are financed by the broadcasting licence, the cost of which is determined by the government. The BBC is not, however, a 'state' institution but an independent body with a policy of impartiality. As a one-time director-general, Sir Hugh Greene, put it, 'We have to balance different points of view in our programmes but not necessarily within each individual programme.'

The BBC began radio broadcasting on 14 November 1922 and experimental television broadcasting started on 30 March 1930. Later that year, on 14 July, the first play was shown on this experimental service. It was a stage play by Pirandello, *The Man with a Flower in his Mouth*. It is quite possible, even probable, that it was the first play televised in any country. Six years later saw the start of regular television programmes, from Alexandra Palace in north London. The first drama was another stage play, *Marigold*, performed in a studio version. The BBC Television service continued until the outbreak of war in 1939 (stopping abruptly, without explanation, in the middle of a cartoon) and in that period the programme organiser was Cecil Madden, who coined a slogan, 'a play a day'. His aim was not achieved in 1937, but amazingly there were 123 performances of plays in that year (including repeat performances). These plays varied in length. Many were short and most were stage successes partially adapted for television. However 1937 did see the transmission of the first play written for the new medium. It was by J. Bissell Thomas and was called *The Underground Murder Mystery*. It lasted ten minutes. Apparently there were some attempts to utilise the possibilities of television in these early days. Film of trench warfare was inserted in a production of R. C. Sherriff's play about the First World War, *Journey's End*, and the tempters in T. S. Eliot's *Murder in the Cathedral* became some sort of supernatural spectres.

BBC Television resumed transmission after the war on 7 June 1946 (still, it should be noted, from Alexandra Palace and only to those parts of the South-east that could receive the signal). The *BBC Year Book* for 1947 gives a succinct picture of the state of television drama:

> Among studio programmes, plays have come first in popu-
> larity. Casting a wide net, the producers brought in
> dramas, comedies, thrillers – Shakespeare and Shaw,
> Oscar Wilde and Edgar Wallace. Besides Shaw's *St Joan*,
> Ian Hay's *The Middle Watch*, Eugene O'Neill's *Anna
> Christie*, and many other established successes, demanding
> the utmost resource in studio accommodation, scenery, and
> costumes, viewers saw numbers of plays specially written
> or arranged for television, among them J. B. Priestley's new
> play *The Rose and Crown*, and the well-known stage and
> film story, *Thunder Rock*.[1]

A year later, the policy of the then head of drama (Robert MacDermot) indicated both an awareness of what was feasible and a desire to change the emphasis:

> I knew that it wouldn't be possible – nor, indeed, desirable –
> to concentrate exclusively on new material. I realised that
> the television audience would always need a staple ration of
> 'Shaftesbury Avenue Successes', but I was anxious that, in
> time, these would constitute not more than fifty per cent of
> our total output. . . .
> Of the remaining fifty per cent of plays, it was my aim to

make half of them specially written for the medium and the rest admittedly written originally for the stage or screen but *not yet seen on either*.[2]

In 1949 television reached the Midlands. The Holme Moss transmitter brought television programmes to the North of England in 1951 and from then on BBC Television gradually spread to the rest of the country. In this same period, television drama was still maintained to a large extent by stage successes, broadcast complete with intervals and even warning-bells to announce the start of the second and third acts. As the fifties progressed, the pattern began to alter under Michael Barry, by then head of television drama. Nigel Kneale's science-fiction serial *The Quatermass Experiment* caught the public's imagination and established a demand for original drama. Inevitably the response was *Quatermass II*. This was also the period that saw the start of the ultimately cosy *Dixon of Dock Green*, a series that was not only paternalistic in content but the begetter of many future police series.

With the competition provided by the opening of the ITV network in 1955, the BBC drama output became much more imaginative and the following years saw the rise of the single play and the introduction of umbrella titles such as 'The Sunday Play' and 'Playhouse'. By 1962, the drama department was producing over 300 hours of drama a year (9 per cent of the total television output). *Dixon* was regularly attracting 13 million viewers early on a Saturday evening, *Z-Cars* was nearly as popular mid-week, and this extraordinary supremacy of police stories was further maintained by a series based on Georges Simenon's *Maigret*.

Two years later the BBC's second channel, BBC-2, opened and there was a resulting increase in the drama output. This followed soon upon the arrival of Sydney Newman from ABC Television as the new head of drama (see p. 49). Under Newman, the drama department was subdivided into three sub-departments: Plays, Series and Serials. He introduced 'The Wednesday Play' and created an atmosphere in which boldness was all. A new realism characterised the output, often (and unfairly) tagged as 'kitchen-sink drama'. Newman was also a populist and instrumental in starting up such serials as the science-fiction *Dr Who*, while other popular series, such as *Dr Finlay's Casebook*, were also flourishing.

Under Newman, Shaun Sutton (formerly a director) became head of serials. In 1969 he became head of drama, a post he held for the next twelve years. In the 1981 Fleming Memorial Lecture, he described the achievement of the seventies:

> This was the decade of consolidation and refinement, when the work was sophisticated and polished to a high gloss; when the presentation of drama, film, studio or outside broadcast, gained authority; when what had seemed difficult and adventurous ten years before became normal expectation. The time when drama went out and about, with more and more film, and with entire productions produced on tape-on-location. It was the era when the skills attendant on drama, everything from graphic title sequences to tape post-production, achieved their own new and exciting standards.[3]

In the middle of this decade the BBC was producing just under 500 hours of drama a year (5.8 per cent of the total BBC output). Less prestigiously, it was also transmitting over 1300 hours of imported or cinema series, serials and films.

Besides the three main departments of the BBC Drama Group, there was a steadily growing regional drama department at Birmingham and sizeable departments at Glasgow and Cardiff. A smaller department in Belfast also made notable contributions to the network. Somewhat predictably the national regional departments' output reflects their countries' supposed preoccupations. In 1981, Scotland produced *King's Royal*, a serial story of distilling-folk, while Wales produced *The Life and Times of David Lloyd George*. Even Birmingham's department (called English Regions Drama Department) had a brief to be 'regional'.

BBC Schools Television also made and continues to make a number of dramas, while a considerable drama output is maintained from BBC Children's Television, including the infamous *Grange Hill*, a children's soap opera. With a regular 10 million viewers, it has proved one of the most popular children's programmes on television. Set in a London comprehensive school, it has won awards, become the subject of more than one academic thesis and been applauded for its realism. It has also been branded as 'disgusting', 'disgraceful' and condemned for 'contributing to the destruction of our society'. A Somerset Women's Institute passed a motion demanding an instant end to the programme, and a branch of the National Union of Teachers complained about pupils imitating bad behaviour shown in the serial and urged that it should show 'the good side of school life'. There have also been a few voices protesting that it is not realistic enough.

In addition to the above there is a small number of dramas made by the BBC Open University department (one series of which were made in 1977 at BBC Television's original home, Alexandra Palace).

The BBC's drama output has, like most departments, been subject to cuts in recent years. Even so, at the beginning of the eighties, it still amounted to 460 hours a year (4.8 per cent of the total output), which means the BBC remains by far and away the major single provider of television drama.

ITV

It was in 1952 that the then Conservative government proposed setting up a commercial television channel, independent of the BBC. The Television Act received Royal Assent in 1954 and the Independent Television Authority came into being.

Unlike the BBC, the ITA (later renamed the Independent Broadcasting Authority upon the arrival of commercial radio) does not make programmes. Instead it grants franchises to companies which then have a contract to provide a television service for their area and to make programmes both for that area and for the network. The IBA's function is not merely regulatory. It plays a role in programme-planning and is ultimately responsible for the content and quality of everything that is transmitted on its network. When the Authority first advertised the contracts to provide programmes for the South-east, the Midlands and the North of England, twenty-five applications were received and eventually the franchises were awarded as follows:

Area	*Weekdays*	*Weekends*
London and the South-east	Associated–Rediffusion	ATV
The Midlands	ATV	ABC
The North	Granada	ABC

(ATV = Associated Television.)

The contracts for the remaining regions were advertised and awarded over the following years until the completion of the network in 1962.

The ITV companies obtain their income from the sale of advertising in their region (and from the sale of programmes to other companies and abroad). Out of this income they must pay a rental to the IBA and a levy on profits to the government. It follows that the above four companies, holding the franchises for the major population areas where income from advertising is much higher than in, say, the Borders, rapidly became the most profitable and the most powerful. They also became the main, indeed almost the only, providers of drama on the ITV network (though Anglia Television, the contractor for the East of England, did become a significant contributor).

In the early days of ITV, the plays presented by each of the 'Big Four' were sometimes thought to reflect the images of the companies, as Bernard Sendall noted in his history *Independent Television in Britain*:

ATV's close associations with the commercial theatre led them to revive stage plays and to introduce to television for the first time such stars as Gielgud, Olivier and Redgrave. Granada, with their accent on social purpose, moved in the direction of plays with a message writ large – by such writers as Miller, Wilder and Osborne. A–R were, as always, the useful all-rounder striving, and with considerable success, to demonstrate their omnicompetence. ABC, with only two days of the week in which to make an impression, sought to be 'different', often commissioning

new plays from new writers and putting to work on them
sometimes old-hand directors, like George More O'Ferrall,
and sometimes young enthusiasts, like Philip Saville.[4]

An ABC flagship was 'Armchair Theatre' (a title borrowed from Alfred de Musset's phrase 'théâtre dans un
fauteuil'). Started under the direction of Dennis Vance, ABC's
drama supervisor, it was an anthology of single plays transmitted on Sunday evenings after a particularly popular light-
entertainment show, *Sunday Night at the London Palladium*.
Obviously 'Armchair Theatre' inherited a large audience, and
the BBC Sunday evening schedule at this time was not generally thought to be 'strong'. Even so it was an impressive
achievement for 'Armchair Theatre' to be in the 'top ten' every
week for the first quarter of 1958. Then Vance returned to
directing and a Canadian, Sydney Newman (later to be the
BBC's head of drama) took over 'Armchair Theatre'. Bernard
Sendall has chronicled his contribution to television drama:

In the Canadian Broadcasting Corporation, Newman had
witnessed, and had also contributed to, the remarkable
flowering of the dramatic arts on television in North America, in which new writers, new actors, and new directors had
all played their parts. He also recognised that television was
a mass medium or nothing; that because of cultural in-
equalities most of the audience had little experience of the
theatre but much of the cinema; that television drama
should reflect and comment on the world familiar to the
mass audience. The story goes that Michael Barry, then
head of BBC drama, took Newman to see Osborne's *Look
Back in Anger* at the Royal Court Theatre. That play, with
its unusual worm's-eye view of society and its derisive
radicalism, seemed to Newman the dazzling light on the
road to Damascus; more accurately, it summed up what he
had come to believe about the drama. He had developed the
notion of 'agitational contemporaneity', and *Look Back in
Anger* confirmed his ideas. An outsider in this country, he
found both the country and its problems utterly fascinating.
He wanted to make plain statements to the mass audience –
statements falsified neither by sentiment nor by doctrinaire

beliefs. Within a couple of years of his appointment to ABC he had built up a school of British writers and directors in sympathy with his objectives. His directors included many men of wide experience in film as well as television. . . .

'Armchair Theatre' attracted and increased its audience perhaps not because of the impact of individual plays but rather by the cumulative effect of a generalised creative drive.

By 1963 a fairly steady pattern had been established. 'Armchair Theatre' (ABC) was being transmitted alternate Sunday evenings. In the intervening weeks, ATV showed its version, 'Drama '63' (likewise a series of single plays). Granada produced a series of contemporary plays for Friday nights, while on Mondays 'Play of the Week' was shared by the Big Four and eventually also by Anglia. Anglia Television's attempt to break into the charmed inner sanctum had not been easy, as was described in the company's *First Twenty One Years*:

> Anglia had announced its wish to contribute to ITV's drama production long before it got on the air. . . . The fulfilment of the intention was another matter. The big four companies charged at that time with providing the bulk of networked programmes were between them already making all the drama required in the schedules and had an understandable reluctance to reduce their own output to let in a new and unproved source. However, Associated–Rediffusion eventually agreed to provide time for up to eight Anglia plays a year, provided they were made in its Wembley studios and using its technicians. So it came about that the first-night play was credited as: 'An Anglia Television production networked by Associated–Rediffusion.' Anglia's own technicians were proud enough to want to show that they could handle plays equally well in Norwich, and *Sweet Poison* was made there and proved their point conclusively. Although more plays were recorded at Wembley, Anglia's reputation was soon so well established that it was able to move production permanently to Norwich and present the plays in its own right. Their popularity made this possible.[5]

Anglia's style was traditional. To quote the same company publication,

Firstly, Anglia dramas have good stories. They are neither obscure nor experimental; every one has a beginning, a middle and an end. This reflects the personal taste of Sir John Woolf who has been responsible for the productions from the outset; the majority of viewers appear to share his views.
Secondly, they frequently have big names in the casts.

A third characteristic has been their infatuation with murder stories: *Countercrime, Intent to Murder, Speaking of Murder, Sound of Murder, Better at Murder.* . . . As the above-mentioned executive, Sir John Woolf, has said, 'Anglia plays are for family viewing . . . they have never involved violence.'

For a short while in 1963 a number of other smaller companies were able to contribute to the drama output. 'Thirty Minute Theatre' was a series of short plays produced by Anglia, Scottish Television, Southern Television (the Southampton-based company) and Television Wales and West (Bristol and Cardiff).

So far we have been considering single plays. The output of series and serials was also considerable, as the list for 1963 shows:

Programme	Description	Company	Minutes
The Avengers	Adventure series	ABC	60
Boyd QC	Courtroom series	A–R	30
Coronation Street	Serial (or soap)	Granada	30
Crane	Adventure series	A–R	60
Emergency–Ward 10	Hospital soap	ATV	30
Espionage	Spy series	ATV	55
The Human Jungle	'A psychiatrist's casebook'	ABC	55
Jezebel, ex UK	Human-drama series	ABC	50

Programme	Description	Company	Minutes
Love Story	Anthology of love stories	ATV	60
Man of the World	Adventure series	ATV	55
Maupassant	Adaptations of short stories	Granada	60
No Hiding Place	Police series	A–R	55
The Odd Man	Mystery series	Granada	60
The Plane Makers	Aircraft-factory series	ATV	55
The Saint	Adventure series	ATV	57
The Sentimental Agent	Adventure series	ATV	55
Sergeant Cork	Victorian detective series	ATV	60
24-Hour Call	Medical series	ATV	45
The Victorians	Eight Victorian plays	Granada	60

Thus the pattern developed. Then in 1966 (as obliged) the ITA announced that from July 1968, when the franchises were to be renewed or reawarded, it would be seeking to appoint five major companies (splitting the Northern region into two areas) and appointing seven-day-a-week contractors in all regions except the South-east.

After much competition, Yorkshire Television acquired the contract for that area, Granada became a seven-day-a-week provider for the North-west, ATV became the full-time Midlands company, and the interests of ABC and Associated–Rediffusion were merged into a new company, Thames Television, and awarded the franchise for London and the South-east from Monday morning to 7p.m. on Fridays. Weekend programmes for that region were to be provided by a new company, London Weekend Television. LWT and Yorkshire quickly joined the ranks of the major drama providers.

Following this reorganisation, the 1970s saw a number of changes and developments in the drama output of the ITV companies.

ATV's output of single plays declined, though it still mounted occasional and expensive productions of Shakespeare and plays by writers such as Oscar Wilde. It ran an anthology of plays under the umbrella title 'Love Story', but otherwise concentrated on series such as *Sapphire and Steel, Heartland, Flickers* and the impressive *Edward VII* and the considerably less impressive soap opera, *Crossroads.*

Granada also devoted much energy and many facilities into series and serials (several of them being dramatisations). *Spoils of War, A Family at War, The Mallens* and *Cribb* were all successful in the ratings, while *Brideshead Revisited* proved how lavish and addictive a television serial could be, although it had its critics. Richard Eyre, for example, described it as 'a massive costume soap opera'. Granada also produced a number of single plays in the seventies (although noticeably less than in the previous decade), as well as *Coronation Street* and the low-budget courtroom series *Crown Court.*

Thames Television inherited ABC's 'Armchair Theatre', which retained its standards for a year or two, struggled for survival over two or three seasons more, and was finally put to death in 1973. Since then almost all of Thames's drama resources have been dedicated to series and serials either glamorous (*Edward and Mrs Simpson*) or 'contemporary' (*The Sweeney, Hazell, Danger UXB, Minder* and so on).

London Weekend has broadcast a number of single plays, often under titles such as 'Seven Faces of Woman' or as a season of plays by one author (Dennis Potter). Otherwise it too has concentrated on series and serials, ranging from *Lillie* to *Upstairs, Downstairs* and *The Professionals.* LWT's head of drama, Nick Elliott, has spoken quite frankly about his company's needs:

LWT has very specific needs in drama – all the other companies have seven nights a week, but we have only three, the weekend nights, with greatest advertising potential. So we put on mass-audience long-running series like *The Professionals*, that develop audience loyalty. We're currently finding it quite difficult to come up with a replacement for it. We've found that women tend to watch more on

Friday nights, so that's a good slot for the more romantic series like *We'll Meet Again*; while the prestige productions like Dennis Potter plays generally go out on Sunday nights.[6]

Yorkshire Television produced a number of single plays in the same period, some under the title 'Yorkshire Playhouse', but in recent years it too has concentrated on series and serials, including dramatisations such as *Flambards* (made almost entirely on film) and *The Good Companions*. As David Cunliffe, Yorkshire's head of drama, also admits,

> I used to get half-a-dozen unsolicited scripts a week; now I get half-a-dozen format proposals for book adaptations. And it's always tempting to go for the Hugh Whitemores and Alan Platers rather than for the unknowns. I'm known as the cheapjack, who does the commercial stuff, and most of our output is middle-of-the-road, because that's what audiences want. ... We've been affected by the insidious influence of America, which loves British costume drama, and it always helps to know you can sell a production there.[7]

Yorkshire also produces a soap opera, *Emmerdale Farm*, unusual in that it regularly includes scenes made on location.

To the above must be added the less regular contributions of the smaller companies. Anglia has continued to make occasional and prestigious single plays (usually proven successes in another medium) and a long-running series, *Tales of the Unexpected*. Harlech Television and Scottish Television have also made a number of series and serials, while Southern Television (with *Worzel Gummidge* and other productions) and Tyne Tees have made notable contributions to the children's output.

A new contract period began in 1982. For this period, (of the drama-producing companies) ATV was reconstructed as Central Television and Southern Television lost its franchise to Television South.

Central Television began with good intent. Its director of programmes, Charles Denton, announced that 'We shall make drama programmes which will attempt to break free of

formula.' The company's controller of drama, Margaret
Matheson (once a producer for BBC's 'Play for Today') has
certainly introduced a new realism and a new commitment to
the single play:

> Series do give writers the opportunity to develop something
> at length, but it means less people writing for TV, and less
> opportunity for directors. . . .
>   I want Central to have the reputation of running a writers'
> drama department, where they can be involved in the
> production and trust us with their work.[8]

It will be interesting to see if that commitment will be maintained. In its first two years, Central has certainly screened
plays which could be labelled 'uncompromising'.

From November 1982, the ITV companies had an additional
outlet for their programmes. That month saw the opening of
Britain's fourth television channel, Channel 4. The Channel 4
Television Company is a subsidiary of the IBA. It is funded by
subscriptions from the ITV companies, who, in return, sell
regional advertising slots on Channel 4. With the exception of
a few continuity and preview programmes, Channel 4 does not
make programmes. Instead it buys or commissions them from
the ITV companies and from independent sources.

The Independents

Until the arrival of Channel 4, there had been little opportunity
for the few independent producers to get their work onto the
television screen in this country. The advent of Channel 4
resulted in a whole range of new companies being set up, more
or less overnight. Some were major concerns, subsidiaries of
established companies. Others were two friends, a phone
number and some ostentatious notepaper. All were optimistic,
but, because drama is the most expensive form of television,
few of the independents indicated a readiness to become
involved in its production. There were exceptions, including
two notable ones.

Brookside Productions is a company set up especially to

make a twice-weekly soap opera for the new channel, which paid out £2.5 million for the first year's programmes, and gave another £1 million towards the initial outlay. *Brookside*, very much the brainchild of Phil Redmond (the inventor of *Grange Hill*), is produced in a novel way – actually on the housing-estate on Merseyside in which it is set. Its method of production is described in Chapter 8. A controversial serial, it has been regularly in the top five ratings on Channel 4.

Very different is Goldcrest Films and Television Ltd, one of the biggest independents with (in 1982) £11 million available to finance its projects. Goldcrest has been responsible for cinema films such as *Chariots of Fire* and *Gandhi* and is another example of the way the British film and television industries are moving closer together. From Channel 4, it won a commission to make 'First Love', a series of seventy-five-minute dramas on film. The first of these, *P'Tang, Yang, Kipperbang* by Jack Rosenthal, was set in the forties and told of a shy and awkward adolescent's love for his classmate. It was reputed to have had a budget of £0.5 million and, like the other dramas in 'First Love', was subcontracted out to Enigma Productions Ltd. Enigma is very much the creation of its chief executive, the producer David Puttnam. Puttnam was also responsible for the creation of Goldcrest, which was financed by investment from such diverse institutions as the Post Office, the Coal Board pension funds, Legal and General, and S. Pearson.

Despite Goldcrest's size and success (twelve films or tele-vision plays ready for transmission after not much more than two years in business), Puttnam still felt the place of the independent companies in Britain was not secure. Speaking at the 1983 Television Festival in Edinburgh, he remarked,

It's a joke to talk about independents. What we have is a group of very dependent independents. Until we have true access to the television channels and we throw off the attitude that we have to be controlled, we shall never be independent.

His point was of course that in Britain a production company (such as Goldcrest or Brookside) still needs a 'publisher' (such as Channel 4). By investing in film dramas (which have a much better chance of subsequent cinema and overseas sales than studio-produced plays), Goldcrest sought to find other outlets so as to ensure both continuing financial success and high standards of quality.

Goldcrest and other independents might also look to cable television, video sales and satellite broadcasting – all theoretically offering outlets to the independents. In practice it looks as if it will be many years before cable in particular will be profitable enough to fund major drama productions (although one independent, Limehouse Productions, has talked about making a soap opera for cable distribution). Video sales and rentals seem destined to be confined to previously transmitted or distributed material, and the British satellite channels have been given over to the BBC and ITV. Apart from giants such as Goldcrest and specialists such as Brookside, it seems unlikely that many independent companies will produce much television drama – unless the BBC and ITV networks open their doors to more co-productions.

Co-productions

In his 1981 Fleming Memorial Lecture, Shaun Sutton neatly summarised the reasons for co-productions, their attractions and drawbacks:

Huge productions – like the BBC's *The Borgias* or ITV's *Brideshead Revisited* will never be possible again without the most robust outside investment – indeed, it has not been possible for years – the domestic purse will simply not run to it.

For many years, co-production has helped to stem the rising tide of cost: or preferably, co-financing, with a sleeping partner, who invests a modest sum in the project in return for the right to transmit it in his own area. True co-operation implies more than a sharing of finance – it demands a blending of talents and resources, of the decisions on casting, scripting and direction; and while such double harness production can be made to work, I remain convinced that drama direction is a personal, one man/one woman affair, and that production by committee usually ends in an anaemic compromise. One must adhere to the right – and the impudence – to say to one's co-financer: 'I know that you have generously contributed nearly 50 per cent of the budget, but I must still insist on full artistic control of the casting, writing and direction'. Anyone who can make that stick deserves to succeed.[9]

Tom English, head of BBC co-productions, has spoken explicitly on the subject. 'We in the BBC do not believe in committee production. The BBC prefers to have editorial control.' Thus it was that *Tinker, Tailor, Soldier, Spy* was co-financed with Paramount but produced by the BBC. There have been similar ventures involving ITV companies and co-financiers; and packages have been put together by varied groups of independents, foreign broadcasting-stations and either the BBC, an ITV company or Channel 4.

Co-financing does bring problems over editorial control; it is time-consuming. It does however point a way head. Despite rising costs (and rising expectations on the part of the viewers) it seems that the provision of drama on television can be assured.

3.
The Producer

In the beginning was . . . the writer.

Well, in theory it is possible for anyone to have an idea for a television play, to sit down at a typewriter, to write the play, post it to a television company, have it accepted, even to have it produced and screened. It is rumoured that such a sequence of events has actually occurred. There are those who will say, with straight faces and in public, that that is how new writers do start in television, if not all the time then at least fairly regularly. But it is simply not true to say that that is how most new plays find their way onto the screen. Nor does a new classic serial reach the screen because A. N. Other writes in to a television station saying he has just read and enjoyed *Woodhouse Towers*, a much neglected nineteenth-century novel, and suggesting that he adapt it in twenty-six episodes for showing on Sunday evenings. . . . (Should *Woodhouse Towers* subsequently reach the screen, A. N. Other can bet his last dollar that the plum job of dramatising it for television will go not to him but to an experienced professional just as soon as that same professional has finished the two other serials on which he is now working.) Nor does a glossy new thriller series get into production simply because a rather more clued-up writer's agent submits a laminated prospectus of the proposed series to the head of drama with whom she exchanged a 'Darling, hello!' at a bar in the National Theatre the previous week. No, in the beginning is the producer.

'The producer' is a term television has borrowed from the cinema. In the film industry, it is the producer's job to find a script. Once he has got one, it is called a 'property'. Next, he sets about raising the money necessary to make the film. Then he can employ staff (including the film's actual director) and set the production process in motion. From then on he is in control of budgets, schedules, publicity and all other business-dealings. In a major film studio (say, in Hollywood), the company would be responsible for raising the money and the producer might be their employee, responsible to the studio chief.

Until the mid fifties, BBC Television drama was made by directors, working to heads of departments. With the advent of series, regular slots such as 'The Sunday Play' and especially with competition from ITV, television drama became a more complicated process. One man could not direct a weekly *Dixon of Dock Green* and be responsible for all its planning, commissioning, and so forth. So there came into being the role of the television drama producer.

So far as I know, there is no one job designation which could apply to every production house. Even in a given institution the job of producer can, in some ways, be exactly what the holder makes it. He or she may be a mighty power in the land, handling budgets reaching seven figures. Alternatively, he or she may have allowed the job to diminish to not much more than a tidy but empty office. More than one staff producer has gone a year without actually producing very much, either through indecision or because a failure to shout loudly enough at planning meetings resulted in not winning a budget.

Basically, a producer is responsible (a) to a head of department and (b) for the production of a unit of single plays, a series (or part of a long-running one), or a segment of a serial. The producer will come up with the basic idea or inherit one. It may be a strand of plays about, say, middle-age love. It may be a Russian theatre classic, or a series with which a foreign tourist board might be very helpful during production. It may simply be something that would fit neatly into Studio A. It could be a series with potential overseas sales. . . . The idea does not by any means always occur to the producer as he or she sits behind a desk. The producer may have had it in mind for years or it may be a sudden inspiration gained in the bar; it may grow during freewheeling conversations or meetings with friends or colleagues. But from somewhere comes the idea.

Through a series of planning-sessions it is developed, extended and curtailed. The thirteen-week series about Corsican smugglers will now be about Cornish smugglers and will be recorded not so much on location as in W12; the Russian theatre classic becomes an Ibsen. Eventually the drama department moulds the project to fit its overall plans while the producer tries to protect his or her concept. Next, management approval must be won. This may be through 'offers meetings' in which a drama department makes 'offers' of productions (along with those from other departments) to a network controller. Alternatively, it may be through meetings with programme controllers, sales executives and representatives of higher management. 'Is this the sort of thing our company wants to do and to be seen doing?' 'How much will it cost?' 'What about co-financiers?' 'Will we be able to sell it to the network?' 'And óverseas?' Serious students of the media have frequently tried to analyse the procedures by which productions come to the screen. This can be a fascinating study of the politics of power, of institutions and of money, and their confrontation with creative ideas. By way of summary, all that can be said is that many concepts fail to win acceptance. Those that do win through do so because one person (the producer) or a small group (the producer and his allies) can convince a group of hard-headed television moguls that, 'At this moment, this is a good idea which is likely to prove successful.'

There is an old joke (told in BBC Radio in fact) which goes, 'Question: What do you need to make a programme? Answer: A programme number.'

Acceptance of a proposal brings to a producer one of those magic numbers or its equivalent. For with a number comes a budget, perhaps even production dates, and just possibly a transmission date (which may or may not prove a blessing). Now the producer has the means and authority to turn that original spark of imagination into a can of film or tape.

Of course, at this stage, the producer may also have a script. Obviously this is the case if the production is to be of a stage play. It may also be the case with an original television play. The existence (or approaching completion) of such a script may have been what gave the producer inspiration, enthusiasm and a budget. In this case the writer may be someone highly respected in the business whom the producer had talked into giving him first option on the writer's next script. Alternatively the writer may be a friend, someone with whom the producer had worked happily on an earlier production and who the producer knows has a suitable idea or script waiting for production. In all such cases, where the producer has a script or knows that the author will now rework his draft ideas, the producer must next find a script editor (more of whom later). In all other cases he has still to find the script.

When looking for a single play, it is a foolish producer who does not approach the famous and the brilliant among the smallish body of busy full-time television dramatists. They may not be that busy. They may have a perfectly good script left over from some aborted series 'for the other side' which is exactly right for the new slot. After all, it would be short-sighted not to accept brilliance simply because it has been inside another drama department. If this fails, one might try the same approach to the almost famous and the fairly brilliant among the established television dramatists. One is also likely to bring in the script editor at this stage to help in the search. If the unit of plays is to be six in number and unless the budget is very tight, the search will not be over until nine or ten scripts or potential scripts have been found (and bought). Amazing things can happen to scripts in the course of production. Provided the department can afford them, it is always as well to have something to fall back on in case of accidents—be they technical, legal, political, marital or simply the result of writer's block (a technical term for procrastination).

Finding writers for series (or serials) can be very straightforward. The producer rings up an established writer with a good track record and a reputation for delivering scripts on time. 'Jim! How are you? Good to hear you. How's the mortgage? Look, I've got this studio-based police series. No, it's new. No, no, very little film. . . . Well, no, we haven't actually got a slot for it yet. What about lunch?' Unless the writer has just had a commission to provide the screenplay for a major feature film, he says yes.

With different people, the process will be very different. X, a producer, knows that Y, a writer, is very much in fashion but has not worked with her. Will she be in sympathy with the new project? Better sound her out before saying too much. Lunch is arranged, perhaps in the waitress section of Television Centre's restaurant, perhaps in a French restaurant that's only just opened but it's supposed to be excellent, nothing like it anywhere else in Shepherd's Bush (or Leeds or Birmingham).... Despite a reputation for awkwardness and toughness, Y is greedy for work but not sure what X is after. Y is therefore vague and non-commital. X is wanting commitment, trying to discover if Y is genuine before revealing anything of the theme, style or subject of the proposed series. Nothing is decided. Again it is time to delegate the business of finding a writer and a script to the script editor.

Surprisingly, through a series of contacts, friends, agents and luck a writer is eventually approved by the producer and commissioned. Contracts departments will haggle with the writer's agent over the fee, bringing in the producer again when stalemate is reached, but soon a script will be on its way. Be it a unit of single plays, a series or serial or a dramatisation (the writing of which we shall return to in the next chapter), the producer now relinquishes immediate responsibility for the script. He has other worries, other problems.

First, there is the matter of ensuring that the necessary technical facilities are still available at the time agreed. Outside broadcast units have an uncanny knack of being diverted to Racing at Newmarket just when you thought they were going to be available for a sequence of dawn scenes on the shores of the Wash. Even worse, a disaster such as a General Election can loom unexpectedly on the horizon. That can monopolise studio space and other facilities for weeks. Even more demanding would be Something Royal. No hope of a single cameraman in the week of a wedding.

Also to be gathered together is the production team. First (and most important) is the director. Unlike the producer who is usually on the staff of the production company or at least on short-term contract to produce a specific unit of plays, the director is usually a freelance. He or she will be hired on account of previous work, specific talents and enthusiasms. One director may be known to be especially keen on the work of the writer and to have worked with him or her before, successfully and even amicably. One director may be known to enjoy location video work, another film. One may be known for work on classic serials, another for work on documentary drama. Many producers have a specific director or stable of directors with whom they work regularly. The relationship between producer and director can be like a marriage. Even today, some marriages are happy and even productive.

Depending on the particular marriage, producer alone or producer and director will now set about choosing a designer ('But he *always* does my design. What do you mean, he's working for someone else?'), together with a technical manager, a film cameraman, costume designer, graphics artist, and other key contributors to the creative process.

So far in this chapter we have been discussing mainly the producer's role in setting up a new series or group of plays. So far as an established and long-running serial (such as *Coronation Street*) is concerned, the task of the production office is somewhat different:

> In addition to the overall producer, the office consists of a programme planner (with responsibility for the logistics of production), two storyline writers, a script editor, a biographical record keeper, and secretarial staff. At any one time three directors, with production assistants, working on various stages of the production of a pair of episodes, will be attached to the office. However, in common with the practice in other companies, cameramen, technicians and other personnel are not allocated permanently to the serial.
>
> Every three weeks a story conference is convened to make decisions about the narrative progression of a further six episodes, within the broader framework of a long-term conference held periodically to map out future directions. In attendance at the story conference are the producer, the series planner, the storyline writers and a number of script writers. Plot developments for a three-week period are discussed and proceedings and decisions minuted. The storyline writers then produce the outlines of six episodes based on the decisions of the conference, and these are allocated to suitable writers. Certain writers have established reputations for types of storyline, and this, together

with availability, is used as a basis for allocating episodes. Additionally, some writers are used to handle important narrative moments – a small core group whose knowledge and 'understanding' of the programme has been acquired over a long period of association. Each writer is contracted for a set number of scripts over a set period.[1]

All these people are closely involved in the creative process. All of them work to the producer. It is not particularly fashionable to describe the producer as a creative artist. Often he is seen as the man (or woman) who limits the creative freedom of writer and director (because he has failed to win sufficient money and facilities for the play or because he is the lackey of institutional censors). Yet it remains a fact that in most productions the producer is the initiator, a point made by Anthony Smith in an appendix to the Annan Report on The Future of Broadcasting:

> His situation within the fairly complex processes of broadcasting is always a special one, in that he is working as a kind of 'author' directly inside a manufacturing and distributing process. He is one of a relatively small number of creative professionals performing his work among people with a variety of different skills, many of which would apply equally well in other industrial processes; he, however, is dependent on the machinery and the administration and the scores of people who supply these, to perform a fundamentally intellectual and creative function.[2]

The Script Editor

Has anyone ever said, 'When I grow up, I want to be a script editor'? Probably not: it is a strange, amorphous job.

As we have seen, part of that job is to find a writer. From then on, the script editor is the producer's link with that writer. The script editor will give the writer advice, remind him or her what facilities are available and generally see that 'impossible' scenes do not get into the script. Out goes

SCENE 8.   EXTERIOR. THE BASTILLE. DAY. LONG SHOT,
            ANGRY MOB APPROACHING.

In goes

SCENE 8.   INTERIOR. ROOM IN BASTILLE. DAY. CLOSE UP,
            JULES, A POLITICAL PRISONER, LISTENING TO
            NOISES OFF, A RAY OF HOPE CROSSES HIS FACE.

Writers tend not to like script editors. They get in the way.
They keep the writer from the producer and director. They
prevent the script from expanding to the ninety minutes it
really ought to be to tell the story properly. . . .
    Good script editors are paragons of tact. They may have
written scripts themselves and know the pain suffered by a
writer when his private creation becomes public property,
when something he has worked on alone suddenly becomes a
canvas on which everyone wants to make his mark. Good
script editors offer encouragement to writers, provide enthusiasm and reassurance.
    Script editors are also responsible for the accuracy and
legality of a script. If the play is set in 1975, the hero cannot
drive off in an Austin Metro. If it concerns a doctor who is
having an affair with one of his patients, and who is seen
briefly in Colwyn Bay, then it is the script editor who must
check and double-check that nothing in the script can possibly
be taken as referring to a particular real-life doctor in Colwyn
Bay (or anywhere else). So far as series and serials are
concerned, the script editor has a further responsibility for
continuity. Has the hero ever been a smoker? Did we once say
he had a sister? Is 'that' in character?
    Especially when there is an established team of producer–
writer–director, a script editor may not be necessary. It is not
compulsory to have one. It is simply that on most productions
he or she is a vital member of the team.
    Good script editors grow up into good producers.

4.
The Writer

'*Bill Brand*? That was by Trevor Griffiths.'
    '*Pennies from Heaven*?'
    'Dennis Potter.'
    '*Days of Hope*?'
    'Er . . . Jim Allen.'
So far as British television is concerned, it is the writer who
is remembered (and therefore generally credited) as the begetter of a particular play.
    Turn to the cinema and it is a different matter. The widely
acclaimed feature film *Gandhi* is thought of as being 'by
Richard Attenborough'. As the public consciousness has it,
'He made it.' (Its screenplay was in fact by John Briley.)
Writing in *The Listener* in April 1983, John Wyver neatly
summarised the different assumptions of the public and critics, concerning the making of film and television dramas:

> It is almost a cliché of criticism that both are collaborative
> mediums, where the final achievement is the product of a
> hundred or more skilled workers. Nonetheless, cinema is
> assumed to be a director's medium. From the time of D. W.
> Griffith on, certain commercial directors, such as Hitch-
> cock, have been recognised as the 'author' of each of their
> films. So, too, have the makers of 'art' films like Ingmar
> Bergman. But the dominance of the director, at least in the
> ways films are written or spoken about, really dates from
> the development of the *auteur* theory in French film criti-
> cism of the late 1950s.
>   This critical approach has been rigorously re-evaluated in
> the last 15 years but the assumption of director-as-author

has stuck deep in our film culture. Television drama, in contrast, has always been identified as a writer's medium.[1]

This is probably because, in Britain at least, television drama has its roots in the theatre. Despite occasional fashions for 'directors's theatre' and despite the supremacy of the star actor, critics have always ultimately credited a stage play to its writer, just as the playwright's name almost always appears on the playbill, usually close to the title. True, the names of the stars may appear in larger print, but the writer is clearly identified as the play's originator. 'Credits' on television and in *Radio Times* have perpetuated this custom, not only in the case of the single play but even in series and serials. Consider this entry in *Radio Times* for what is basically a soap opera:

6.40 Angels
by MAUREEN GLADYS CHADWICK
Tony Armatrading as Josh Jones
Michelle Martin as Janet Dickins
Pauline Quirke as Vicky Smith
Juliet Waley as Alison Streeter
Neil West as Dave Nowell
Joy Lemoine as Ayo Ladipo
On a visit to the hospital laundry,
Jean MacEwen's students are
amazed by the scale of it all.

Marie-Laure Bresson.EMMA WATSON
Dick Willoughby......STACY DAVIES
Dolly Fisher...........PEGGY SHIELDS
Ron Cracknall........TERENCE LODGE
Jean MacEwen........CAROL HOLMES
Edward Clarke......JON GLENTORAN
Shirley...................VAL HASTINGS
Kathy Barnham......JULIE BRENNON
Script editor SUSAN HAGAN
Designer STANLEY MORRIS
Producer BEN REA
Director WILLIAM SLATER
(*Next episode on Thursday at 6.40 pm*)

Courtesy *Radio Times*

Compare the layout of that entry with one for what is also a soap opera (albeit a glossier one), shown on the same evening:

8.10 pm *New series*
Dallas

blazes back to the screen
starring
Larry Hagman as J. R. Ewing
Patrick Duffy as Bobby Ewing
Linda Gray as Sue Ellen Ewing
Victoria Principal as Pam Ewing
Charlene Tilton as Lucy Ewing
Steve Kanaly as Ray Krebbs
Susan Howard as Donna Krebbs
Ken Kercheval as Cliff Barnes
Howard Keel as Clayton Farlow
Timothy Patrick Murphy as
Mickey Trotter
John Beck as Mark Graison
The Road Back
J.R., Sue Ellen, John Ross and Ray
are trapped by a raging fire in the
Southfork mansion . . . The tragic
news has a devastating effect on
Miss Ellie . . . Lucy keeps a vigil
by Mickey's bedside as the doctors
battle to save his life. Who will
survive the Southfork inferno?
Will recent events finally decide
the burning question of who will
own Ewing Oil?

Written by ARTHUR BERNARD LEWIS
Directed by NICK HAVINGA
★ *Subtitles on Ceefax page 170*

Courtesy *Radio Times*

The reason for the difference stems presumably from the fact
that *Angels* is of British origin while *Dallas* is American. As
we have seen, in America television drama owes more to the
cinema than to any other medium, both for its origins and for
its working-methods. Consequently there it is far more usual
to think of the director rather than the writer as the 'maker' of
the television play (which is in practice usually a film
anyway).

Much has been written and said in the debate as to whether
this *auteur* theory (see John Wyver, above) is valid. A truly
awe-inspiring body of criticism has been written in support of
the director-as-author argument; nearly as much by those
who champion the writer (or, less fashionably, the producer)
as 'author' and by those who insist that a film is the product of
collaboration.

I suspect that much of the critical support for any argument which wants to credit one single person as originator is born of romanticism rather than being grounded in logic. In a natural desire to see film as an art form, we try to make it fit in with our preconceptions that a work of art must be 'pure', the unsullied product of a genius, an individualist, working alone to express his or her vision. Any collaborative process would smack of compromise, 'art by committee' or perhaps commercialism. If a film has a single maker, then it is much easier to accept it as 'Art'. That acceptance also makes it worthy of academic and critical study. Is it too cynical to suggest that critics who advance the *auteur* theory do so out of a vested interest?

For similar reasons there is a desire to preserve the status of the writer as the one and only originator of the television play. To some extent this is a conspiracy between critics and writers. The former (though serious television critics are comparatively few in number) have the same vested interest as their film counterparts, while writers have a natural desire to preserve the status, respect and authority that they collectively remember from the theatre and early days of television (whether or not they worked in either).

Obviously there have been and still are plenty of cases (particularly of single plays) where the writer deserves the credit as sole originator. Virgin births are not the rule however. Producers, directors and many others have sufficient influence on the creative process for them to be able to say when a play is screened, 'I helped to create that.' We shall consider the role of the director in detail in the next chapter. It is relevant to point out here that (with the exception of a few special cases, such as one or two tightly-knit and lasting partnerships) before the director arrives on the scene the script exists at least in the womb even if it has not been delivered.

From the last chapter, it will be clear that I see the role of producer as a creative one: he or she does more than provide space, time and money. In the case of series and serials, the producer may be the initiator of the concept. Even in the case of a single play, the producer may start the creative process.

'I'm thinking of a series of single plays on the theme of power.'

'Power?'

'Yes. Interested?'

'Well . . . How are you defining power?'
'That's up to you. You're the writer. You know, governmental, personal, within an institution, local authority—'
'Local authority?'
So whose idea is the resulting play on the power exerted by a district councillor on his neighbour?
We must accept the cliché that television is a collaborative medium.
How then does the writer fit into this collaboration? Unhappily, according to many writers; happily, according to those who have accepted the nature of the process, as Julian Mitchell, a novelist and playwright, and now also a television playwright, has done:

> Of course I sometimes longed to be the sole arbiter of my own work again. But in any collaboration – and the number of collaborators in television is as large as in film, if not larger – you have to surrender absolute autonomy. Isolation and loneliness, though, are surrendered, too. If you've been on your own for years, to be part of a team, and generally acknowledged the most vital part, is a profound pleasure. And you are so acknowledged, because television is the opposite of film; the word is supreme over the picture, and the vast majority of TV directors aim to serve the script not themselves. There are exceptions, of course; particularly among those who've made their living in advertising and are on their way to Hollywood.[2]

That passage is taken from an essay called 'Television: An Outsider's View'. Julian Mitchell makes the point that, although the writer is recognised as a vital member of the creative team, he is also an outsider. Unlike the producer (who has an office, a secretary, a pension and – as Mitchell points out in the same essay – that supreme mark of status, a parking-space), the writer is a visitor in the building. Unlike the director, who is hired to tell people what to do, he has no real authority. Unlike the technicians, who are on the staff and overtime, he does not know his way around. Unlike the actors, he is alone.
Very few television stations in this country have ever had

staff writers (as opposed to script editors). However, most television drama is written by professional writers. That is, by full-time, freelance writers who specialise in film and television. They may be known to concentrate on single plays or they may be of that body of known, proven professionals from whom producers feel it is safe to commission an episode of a series or serial, secure in the knowledge that it will fit the brief, be of about the right length and possibly arrive on time.

The established theatre dramatist or novelist might also feel moved to try his (or her) hand at a script for 'the box'. If he (or his agent) is of any standing or has his wits about him, the submitted script will follow a chat over drinks or at least a phone conversation to check that it will be read by someone likely to be sympathetic. If the writer is of any standing, then the producer may well indicate a readiness to make a decision on a synopsis or treatment, plus a number of scenes.

As has been said earlier, the 'amateur' is free to write and submit a play. Many do. Some such scripts are accepted. Indeed there are many established and highly regarded writers who have begun this way, writing exactly what they felt impelled to write and maybe only that. They have survived endless rejections, persisted and won through. If, however, you are looking for some sort of career structure in the business of writing television drama, then you are far more likely to find that the established writer developed basic skills in other forms of writing (journalism, novels, theatre, and so on) and then broke into television by way of serials. More than one letter has been written on the lines of, 'Dear Sir, Enclosed is a specimen script for an episode of your serial, *Seaport*. I know you will not be able to use it, but I thought you might like to see it as an example of my work. . . .' And, if the enclosed script has shown an understanding of the genre, the serial in question (and its budgets, restrictions, and so forth), then that writer may well be invited to a meeting, asked for further trial scripts and possibly given a commission.

The writing of scripts for a long-running serial is sometimes scorned: 'Hack work!' It must be admitted that the parameters of the serial may be such that the writer has little freedom to be genuinely original, but it is nevertheless skilled and demanding work. It teaches the writer a lot about the medium, about the structure of an episode, about the way in which an audience can be held. It is incidentally worth looking at the credits of established television playwrights and noting how many now illustrious names have (and are often proud to have) a batch of episodes for *Coronation Street* or *Z-Cars* to their name.

Obviously the potential writer must have some understanding of the medium. He must appreciate that a script which demands two hundred extras, the Hanging Gardens of Babylon and a flood is not one that will be readily accepted; but he does not need, for example, a detailed knowledge of video-editing and dubbing. Indeed, an excessive preoccupation with technicalities can get in the way of his creative work. His job is, after all, to produce a story. To do this, he needs that unteachable asset, a dramatic instinct. He needs to be able to write natural dialogue, to communicate necessary information without too many lines like 'Forsooth, Mistress Mary, are you not worried for the safety of your brother Sir Launcelot, while he is away fighting the cruel Saracens and it all uncertain that he be home for Christmas, which, lawks a-mussy, will soon be upon us and us with no money to buy a goose?' The writer must also know how to build a scene, to develop tension subtly, how to make a character credible and sympathetic (or otherwise) and how to pace a script (i.e. how to develop urgency and excitement, to know when it is time for a reflective interlude, and the like). Even the best-staged car chase can be maintained for only so long. There comes a time when we must be allowed to stop and think along with the characters.

The writer must be aware that television is an intimate medium. An unending succession of panoramic views is as boring as a collection of picture postcards seen across a room. Television drama demands that we meet people, and in close-up. But television is also fluid. We can move from place to place, not as cheaply as we can in radio drama, but so much more easily than can stage drama. The writer needs to be able to exploit this facility – a script which could just as easily be performed on radio or on stage will usually seem odd on television (at least to the director).

Consequently, the writer must have a visual sense. It is all too easy to think that, because a printed playscript looks as though it is mainly dialogue, plays are nothing but conversation. The television writer is not writing for publication. He is writing for those who will make the play happen. It is therefore quite enough to write: 'C. U. MURIEL. SHE HAS BEEN LYING.' Camera and actress will convey that information quite adequately. There is no need to write unreal dialogue to thump the information home.

All this said, an awareness of the grammar of television is nothing without ideas. Most of all, the writer needs to concentrate on content, on his narrative, on what he wants to say.

Obviously it is impossible to generalise about what gives a writer a first idea for a play, just as it is impossible to generalise about what makes a poet or painter begin a particular composition. The playwright's starting point may simply be a chance remark overheard in a pub or on a bus. It may be a photograph in a magazine. It may be a sudden insight or a long-held inner conviction. It may be a sudden awareness that a particular situation would be intrinsically comic, or it may be a storyline handed to him by the script editor of a series or serial. Each play begins in its own way.

Tom Clarke, the author of a biographical play, *Mad Jack*, which is about the First World War poet Siegfried Sassoon, based his script on letters, poems, and an interview with the poet. It also resulted from a personal experience. Having been at one of the Grosvenor Square demonstrations in 1967, Clarke decided he wanted to comment on the nature and effectiveness of an individual's protest against 'the system'. The result was a play that was both a moving story of one man's protest (against the follies of the First War) and a telling comment on what happens when an individual comes into conflict with a hierarchy. It was as relevant in 1967 as it would have been fifty years earlier.

In his book *Making a TV Play*, the late C. P. Taylor has described a similar starting-point:

As a socialist never knowing how one could possibly achieve a socialist revolution in Britain, I had promised myself, for years, to look in detail into several revolutions in the past, to see how they had been achieved. I believed there was something of the superman in Cromwell, Lenin and Castro that enabled them to bring about their revolutions.

If I could sell the idea of a trilogy about revolution to somebody, I would be paid for exploring territory I had long wanted to explore.

Thirty Minute Theatre had been asking me to write something for them for some time. Towards the end of December, I wrote a short outline of the central idea of the trilogy and sent it to the BBC:

'REVOLUTION'

Outline of three plays on revolution for Thirty Minute Theatre

> *The theme of the trilogy is the role of the individual in revolution. It will look closely at three great revolutionaries – Cromwell, Lenin and Castro, during the particular turning points of their revolutions . . . The first play, I have titled,* AT WINDSOR, *the second*, RETURN TO PETROGRAD *and the third* ON SIERRA MAESTRA.

(I subsequently suggested these titles were rather coy and we should get down to brass tacks by calling spades spades. The final titles were, in fact – CROMWELL AND CHARLES, LENIN, CASTRO.)[3]

Not only historical scripts will involve research, as another distinguished television writer, David Cook, has recorded:

Many of the plays I myself have written for television have a medical or social theme. I've spent a night in Casualty at the Birmingham Accident Hospital and spent days with brain-damaged patients being taught a trade. I've been on courses for Marriage Guidance Counsellors, visited a Salvation Army Detoxification Unit for Alcoholics, helped in a School for Autistic Children. 'Write about what you know', is good advice, but it can restrict you to writing about a very small area of life. 'Know about what you write', is better, because then you set out for yourself to find out about what you don't know.[4]

The good writer will take his research seriously whether it is
for what he hopes will prove a prestigious single play or an
episode of a series (although in the latter case a script editor or
production office may provide a lot of background information). Almost any period of thorough research will provide
more information than can be used. That is proper: the writer
needs to know more about Cromwell or a Salvation Army
Detoxification Unit to write the play than his audience does to
appreciate it. This however does present the problem of
selection, which can be very painful. Having spent four weeks
studying the activities of candidates, their wives, agents,
party helpers and all those involved in an election campaign, I
have been most reluctant to ditch many a fascinating detail
that nevertheless held up the plot. Having researched the
history of a family and become steeped in its eccentricities I
have felt a great urge to include every squabble I found
recorded in the diaries.

The process of finding a story (or fleshing out a given one);
of living with its characters in your head until you know
exactly how each one behaves and talks and reacts; of vis-
ualising possible and probable scenarios; of selecting and
editing, shaping and phrasing; of drafting a first version and a
second; of rewriting, of angrily throwing unpleasing speeches
into a waste-paper basket; of typing and retyping – all this is a
long and lonely (very lonely) process. But eventually a script
is completed and posted off. It goes through the stages to be
described in later chapters. Eventually it is recorded on tape or
film. Inevitably it is not quite what you intended. It is shown
to the press and the public. A few columnists write clever
witticisms about it in the quality Sunday papers and the
millions watch, perhaps while eating, dozing or chatting.
And, to quote an anonymous writer quoted by Julian Mitchell,
'If only the buggers would send an occasional postcard!'[5]

So why write for television?

Many write because of what they want to say. It may be to
make a political or social statement, to communicate a per-
ceived truth. That, according to Sir Huw Wheldon in his 1976
Richard Dimbleby Lecture, is the prime business of the (television) play:

It can provide pleasure, of course, and delight, and insight; but its main concern is the exploration of truth. The truth of a news bulletin is the degree to which it accurately describes an event that has taken place. The truth of a play is not so different. It is the degree to which it accurately describes a world conceived inwardly. It is the degree to which that world, inwardly conceived, has been accurately embodied. The degree to which it is not meretricious. The degree to which it hangs together as a single object, cutting no corners, cheating no one, including the author.[6]

If you do have a truth you wish to communicate, why not choose the most popular medium, television? If that shrewd theatrical operator, Shakespeare, were alive now, would he be writing for a repertory theatre or a television company? Obviously, if you have a message to share then television is an obvious medium to choose if you have the option. Why speak to fifty people in a fringe theatre if you can catch 4 million on BBC-1?

There are other reasons for writing. There are those writers who have uncluttered desire to entertain, to tell a plain (or devious) tale as entertainingly and as grippingly as possible. There are those who have a genuine desire to bring glamour and excitement into the domestic situation. There are those (apparently few in number) who have a desire to provoke laughter.

But there are other reasons too for writing. Television drama is close to 'show biz'. It has a glamour, a mystique, a freemasonry that is comforting to the initiate. The pleasure of being hailed by name across the BBC Club by an executive producer can sustain many a writer during weeks of isolation at the typewriter. Additionally, there is the gratifying comfort that millions are watching your work. Then there is the pay.

It goes without saying that television dramatists are ripped off cruelly by penny-pinching managements, but the following tables (1983 figures) give some indication of the basic rewards to an established writer for a first transmission of a play:

	BBC	*ITV*
60-minute play	£3450	£3800
50-minute episode of a series	£2450	£3000
50-minute episode of a serial	£2450	£2400–3800
30-minute episode of a serial (storyline provided)	–	£998
50-minute dramatisation	£1850	£2250

Viewed as payment by the minute, such fees look generous. As payment for weeks of research, writing and rewriting (as first the script editor and then the director comes up with additional 'good ideas'), and when the overall investment in a play and the size of the audience are taken into account, then the rewards are not quite so generous. (The above fees may be no more than 2 per cent of a play's total budget.) The figures also illustrate the hierarchy that exists within the world of television drama: at the bottom the lowly serial, at the top the single play. What the figures do not immediately reveal is that a far more comfortable living can be made from contributing to serials or from dramatisations than from writing original plays. It will be a very lucky or distinguished playwright who has three or even more single plays transmitted in any one year. The experienced (and therefore regularly employed) so-called 'hack' or dramatiser may easily win two or three commissions in a year – each of several episodes.

When a writer is commissioned to dramatise a novel for television, he or she will be told by the producer not only the book (i.e. he does not have to come up with the idea) but also the number of episodes, how much of it will be made on location and how much in the studio, and he may be told who will be the director. It is then up to him to go away and turn one art form into another. This is not as easy as it might seem. It is far more than copying out the dialogue and writing, 'L. S. HENCHARD WALKS ACROSS EGDON HEATH.'

The dramatiser must soak himself in the novel, absorb its

moods and themes, its style and of course its characters. He has a duty to the book and to the novelist but he does not owe them blind obedience. He has an equal duty to the medium of television: indeed, he is very much the servant of two masters. It helps if he can see where the novel's weaker passages are and can maintain confidence in his own ability to write a television play that is as good as the novel.

In the actual shaping of his serial, he must ensure that each episode has a strong ending. Such points are unlikely to come at regular intervals in the novel and he may have to rearrange certain scenes in order to give the episode a dramatic structure. All the time he must bear in mind how many settings and locations he can use – and keep within those limitations. He must also be aware of limits on the size of the cast, not only for budget reasons. Novels are often overpopulated with characters who drift into view briefly, only to disappear for ten chapters. Such characters can overcrowd the small screen and a television audience does not easily remember or re-accept a character who has been absent for four episodes. All this may mean fairly drastic pruning or even the removal of entire subplots.

Obviously some dialogue can be lifted straight from the novel, but much that looks acceptable and in period on the page of a classic novel will serve only to 'corpse' the actors with hysterics when they try to say it in rehearsal. Other novels contain little dialogue. A notable example is *I, Claudius*, for which its dramatiser, Jack Pulman, had to invent almost all the lines. At the other end of the scale, ponderous speeches can be replaced with a quick reaction shot. Harder problems to resolve are lengthy daydreams or passages in which the novelist explores the inner life of a character. Here the dramatiser must know just how much he can rely on director, actors and, for example, music to convey the necessary effect. Not everything need be put on paper, though obviously the wise dramatiser will keep in mind those for whom he is writing and put on paper what they need to know.

Eventually, the script will be written. By now a director will have been appointed. It is time for the script to go into production.

As has been implied earlier in this chapter, for many writers the collaborative process of production is an unhappy one. This is perhaps more likely to be the case when the script is a single play. For weeks this has been the private concern of the writer, it has been prompted by personal convictions and inner imaginings. Deep in his own mind, it has the status of a work of art. More than that, as Ian Curteis has pointed out, both legally and morally its copyright belong to the author.

No wonder then that the writer wants to be closely involved in all subsequent stages. My own view is that, where this does not happen, it is not because of some sinister and imperialist policy perpetrated by the producing organisation but the result of a clash of personalities (usually between director and writer). Such clashes happen. Directors get labelled by writers as 'cavalier', 'unsympathetic' and 'arrogant'. Writers become known as 'difficult'. It is not surprising then that writers have made many attempts to institute a code of practice which all producing organisations would force directors to observe, in order to safeguard their work.

Some of the points writers would like to see enshrined in all contracts include the right:

(1) to be notified of all rehearsals, recordings and post-production schedules (and of any changes to such schedules);
(2) to be consulted on the casting of all principal characters;
(3) to have access to all rehearsals (and to be paid an attendance allowance and expenses);
(4) to be invited to any press previews; and
(5) to be informed of the dates of all transmissions, including repeats, and of any changes to transmission times.

Some writers would also wish to insist on access to all editing sessions and to be involved in discussions about scheduling. In return, most would allow such qualifying clauses as the writer agreeing not to guarantee an actor a part in a play and not to communicate directly with cast or technical crew without the producer's or director's approval.

How you react to such points will depend on your sympathies. The above points may seem very fair. Why should his script not remain under a writer's control? Why should managements be allowed to get away with a bland, 'But it's really not practicable, is it?' Yet one must also sympathise with a director who is trying to draw the best performances out of his cast also having to cope with a writer who is fuming or sulking because the leading man is blond and not swarthy, because the leading lady is North-country and not a Midlander; and because a line has been altered. Then there is the well-known fact that, the more people there are in an editing-suite, the slower the editing.

The rights of authors surfaced once again at the Edinburgh Television Festival in 1983. One writer, Fay Weldon, spoke passionately of the triumvirate of producer, director and script editor together with the weight of the producing organisation behind them ranged against the poor writer. She objected to the use by directors of such phrases as 'unjustified paranoia' whenever a writer complained. In the same debate, Ian Curteis (see above) also lamented how 'the noble concept of one person's mind has dwindled to formula work; safe, mechanically clear and unwatchable'. In the same debate, Piers Haggard spoke in defence of directors. He rejected an analogy of the director being a violinist performing a composer's score. 'In a good director's hands other things develop – silences, movements. . . . Drama does not live by words alone.'

Others spoke of the need for 'unity', the need for directors and writers (both freelances within institutions) to co-operate to defend a form (i.e. the single play and indeed all prestigious television drama) from attack by commercial pressures and censors. At least one speaker pointed out that there were rewards to be gained from team work. Julian Mitchell has also noted the benefits to a television script of consultation:

> As a result of all this close reading and re-writing, most television scripts are far better written, far better constructed, than most novels. It is just that much harder to get away with self-indulgence, flabby prose, padding, inconsistency, implausibility.[7]

But that does not mean he feels the writer has no reason or right to be present at rehearsals:

When I began, some directors tried to keep me away from rehearsals, and in my ignorance I did go away, and had no one but myself to blame when things went wrong which I could have prevented. The writer has every right and reason to be present during all stages of the making of his play. How much time he actually spends on it will depend on the trust he has established with his director and producer.

It is a large part of the producer's job to see that that trust does develop between writer and director (even though he may be jealous of their relationship). Any clashes of temperament are to some extent his fault for matching the wrong director with a particular writer. When the match is right, the collaborative and creative process can continue amicably, with director and writer happy to listen to each other. However, once the script has been accepted, the burden passes to the director.

1a The studio set for the interior of 'The Rover's Return' in Granada's *Coronation Street.*

1b An early method of 'fading to black': Lance Sieveking, the producer of the first televised play, *The Man with a Flower*, wields the fading board.

2a Carol White as Cathy and Ray Brooks as Reg in the famous documentary drama *Cathy Come Home.*

2b On location in the Royal Shakespeare Theatre, Stratford-upon-Avon: the BBC recording of *The Wars of the Roses.*

3a Light, special effects and space being used to create a scene in a BBC television production of *Hamlet*.

3b The studio set for the BBC Television production of *The Tempest* in 1979.

4a The *Brookside* close.

4b The Downing Street set built for Yorkshire Television's *Number Ten*.

5a The permanent outdoor set for Granada's *Coronation Street*.

5b Rigging lighting on location.

6a On location: the actor Kenneth More receives attention to his make-up from Anglia Television's make-up supervisor, Audrey Mos.

6b Actors Cyril Cusack and Rod Taylor check their lines while filming on location.

7a Lighting, camera crew and the P.A. wait to record a running shot.

7b A running shot, which involves a mobile sound crew in Anglia
Television's *Tales of the Unexpected*.

8a Preparing to film a stunt scene on location in Anglia's *Tales of the Unexpected*.

8b For the same episode of Anglia's *Tales of the Unexpected*, a car is rigged to film both occupants of a car. Note the number of support vehicles on the location.

9a & 9b Just occasionally, the cast considerably outnumbers the crew, as when Granada filmed the meet of the Marchmain Hounds in *Brideshead Revisited*.

10a Inside a scanner: vision mixer, John Bourne.

10b Inside a scanner: an engineer checks picture quality.

11a Inside a scanner: Sid Denney, Anglia's Head of Sound, fades a sound channel.

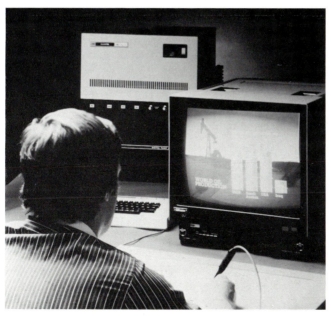

11b Using the Quantel paintbox to create graphics.

12 Jonathan Miller at a producer's run.

13a & 13b Actress Sian Phillips during a complicated make-up session with make-up artist Norma Hill.

14a The sound boom operator keeps the microphone close to Louie Ramsay and James Bolam while recording a scene for BBC Television's *When the Boat Comes In*.

14b In the studio: the floor manager supervises the recording of a scene in 'The Rover's Return' of Granada's *Coronation Street*.

15b A post-production video suite.

15a One- and two-inch videotape recorders in a VT suite.

16a An 'off-line' editing suite from Lane End Productions.

16b Future practice? A combined camera-recorder from Denman Video Productions in use on location in Portugal.

5.
The Director

'What do we call a person who says "Cut to Camera 3" a second after the vision mixer has cut to Camera 3?'
'A director.'
'In television, when anything goes wrong, who was not to blame?'
'The director.'
'In a television studio, who is God?'
'The director.'

No more than would-be jokes – but whose name appears last on the roller caption at the end of a play and stays on screen longest?

The director's.

The director is in charge. It is his job to interpret the script, to see that what is seen on the screen reflects the writer's intentions. It is his job to understand the play (its plot, structure, characterisation, background and themes). It is (in part) his job to cast the play; it is his job exclusively to guide, encourage and help the actors. It is his job to link the work of the designers, the lighting-engineers and those in charge of sound, music and the studio floor. It is supposedly his job to keep within the budget set by the department and it is his job to provide the viewer with as high a standard of entertainment as possible. He must entice, coax, mould, weld a huge number of talented, opinionated artists and craftsmen into a single unit that will make a play. It is of course a most agreeable job.

It is very difficult to say where directors come from. Some have worked in the theatre, a few in radio. Some have been script editors. Many get their first break directing a couple of cameras at a storyteller in a children's television programme.

Many have been trained by the BBC. Almost all are freelance. The best direct only the plays they choose to direct.

As the mythology has it, the director (say he is called Simon) is at home when the phone rings. It is his old friend Jonathan, a producer. Jonathan wonders whether Simon is busy in, say, March. Would he like to have a look at a script Jonathan is sure he won't be able to resist. Jonathan tells him a little more and Simon agrees to have a look at it. It arrives by post the next morning. As he has nothing in his diary for next March, Simon decides it is exactly the sort of play he feels is right for him to direct at this stage of his career. There are things he will want to do to the script and the budget is not big enough, but, yes, it is the sort of challenge he rejoices in.

Despite the fact that the writer has already had to take his script through several drafts in order to satisfy the producer, it is time for a meeting between director and writer in order 'to iron out a few little difficulties'. The writer may be weary of revising his play, the producer and script editor may resent the suggestion that they have not yet got the script into a state of perfection, but the director does bring a new eye to bear on what everyone else has been living with for weeks, and he may well have some sensible suggestions. It is a time for diplomacy.

In John Challen's play *Lifelike*[1] an ex-teacher, Martin, has written what he thinks is a realistic view of a comprehensive school. In this excerpt he is being questioned about his script by the director, Andrew, and the producer, Neil:

NEIL. The language there, Martin . . . how true to life?

MARTIN. In my experience, absolutely so.

NEIL. You're the one who knows. I did . . . (*he was going to say 'wonder'*) well, such a stream of . . . obviously, it's right outside my experience. And kids, nowadays, they really do?

MARTIN. Yes. That type of kid, certainly.

NEIL. Even in those circumstances?

MARTIN. Oh yes.

ANDREW. Fair enough. I'm not backing off, don't think that. Just — I'm afraid we shall have to tone it down a bit. Well — a bit. A good deal. Circumstances being what they are. Not censorship, you understand, but — well, I needn't elaborate, I'm sure. Which doesn't mean we're not going hard for authenticity. Quite the contrary.

NEIL (*to* MARTIN). Which is why we're going to have to rely on you a lot.

ANDREW (*also to* MARTIN). Too true. I must say, I was distinctly relieved when Neil told me you'd be able to be around from time to time. We've got to get it right. So people can't just sit back and think. 'Well maybe, maybe not . . .' They've got to think: 'This is it.'

There are other meetings. Producer and director discuss at length what money and facilities are available, with the producer insisting on keeping within the budget and the director keen to mount a production that will be sufficiently lavish to attract attention throughout the business and win him a reputation for doing things with flair and style. At this stage, producer and director also talk about casting – and possibly involve the writer. If the production is part of a series or serial, most of the main characters will presumably be already cast. The director has a freer rein when it comes to casting those characters who appear only in the episode he is to direct. In the case of the single play, the producer will still expect to have some say in the casting, but here it is largely the director's prerogative.

The director John Glenister reckons that 80 per cent of the success of a production lies in getting the casting right. Another director, Tristan de Vere Cole, has noted his thoughts on the casting process (when working on C. P. Taylor's play *Charles and Cromwell*; see p. 75):

In casting, one had a certain amount of leeway with Cromwell – conflicting portraits and descriptions – perhaps a general impression in the public's mind of a 'solid' man. With Charles, however, the public have a firm 'Van Dyck' image and I felt strongly we should adhere to this.

I was very happy that Leslie Sands was very keen to do it. In my letter to him, I suggested he should play it as 'sent' as possible. This, in conjunction with his own physical force and 'Ironside's' face, I felt, would make a splendid Cromwell.

Although only 32, I was confident Kenneth Colley could

take the necessary make up and, apart from looking re-markably like Charles, I felt he could 'act' him. (One of my faults, in the eyes of friends, was that I did not make him arrogant or proud enough. Having settled to play the public's image of Charles, I think, perhaps, this is fair comment).[2]

The wise director also gives plenty of thought to how the cast will get on with each other. He should think very carefully before asking someone to play a love scene with an ex-partner or with someone he or she cannot abide. He must also take into account (necessarily but unfairly) what other work the actor has been doing recently. A detective from a long-running series may look hopelessly comic in doublet and breeches.

By now the producer will have booked rehearsal rooms, outside broadcast facilities (i.e. the actual machinery needed for recording) and the studio. He may also have booked a designer (brave to do this without consulting the director), costume designer, make-up designer, lighting-supervisor and post-production facilities. From now on, though, the producer will be less in evidence and it is up to the director to liaise with those responsible for the various aspects of design. In these meetings he outlines his thoughts about the way he sees the play – its mood, tone and period. He must give some idea of the cast he is hoping to assemble (their physical characteris-tics can influence design considerably) and talk about the images he hopes to achieve on the screen. In return, the specialists he meets will each contribute their own ideas.

There may also be time for outings, known as research:

The designer and I went to Windsor to research – had splendid day but didn't glean much of use from the most helpful Royal Librarian. Charles' apartments and Chapel would have been built by Edward Third and we decided to base our sets on that period, with Stuart overtones.

I also visited Kensington Gardens Museum where I got the idea of Charles having a watch. I also thought that Charles' dogs should be something an audience could latch on to.

It is impossible to generalise about how long this 'working up' period lasts. In the case of *Charles and Cromwell* it was four weeks. For a classic serial, it will be much greater. With a long-running serial, the process will resemble more a production line, as is the case with *Coronation Street* (where incidentally the directors tend to be members of Granada's staff and not freelances):

Each director is given three weeks to bring the scripts into recorded episode form. The first task is the preparation of a camera script – indicating shot type and camera use, camera deployment in sets etc., for each scene. Set deployment in the studio has to be mapped out. Rehearsal and recording take place in the third week. Monday is used for the recording of any outside scenes – usually on electronic cameras in the Street set near the Manchester studios, although occasionally using film cameras in other parts of Manchester; while Tuesday and Wednesday are taken up with rehearsals. Studio recording of the two episodes is done on Thursday afternoon and all day Friday, moving from set to set rehearsing then recording each scene on electronic cameras. On some occasions several takes are necessary, but the restrictions of time deter unnecessary delay. Technical problems or actor fallibility were more of a hazard when the episode was recorded in one continuous take. The final takes for each scene are edited together in half a day with the director in the week after the recording. The episodes are transmitted two weeks later.[3]

On a production of any size, the director has an assistant. He or she may be dispatched to seek out suitable locations on which to film or record outdoor scenes – for example, to negotiate with a local education authority over the use of a school building during the school holidays or with a railway preservation society over the use of its track and trains in a Victorian serial. The first is hard: the education authority will want to know if there are any acts of vandalism, drugs or swear words in the script. The second is easy: such use brings valuable publicity as well as a 'facilities' fee. It is actually surprising how ready owners of period houses, gracious parkland, museums, and so forth, are to hire out their properties to television companies intent on disguising them as something slightly different.

The director is meantime completing the casting process. For some roles, he may hold auditions or (quite frequently these days) have a look at video cassettes of actors' recent work.

All the time he is playing a sort of vast three-dimensional chess game in his mind, building up images of how 'it' will look on the screen. At this stage, only he (and the writer, producer and script editor) have any overall vision of the finished product (and their visions are quite likely to be wildly different). The director will be thinking not only in pictures, but also in sounds (dialogue, sound effects, music) and in terms of what will be effective cuts, fades and dissolves, when a close-up will tell us all we need to know, when a long shot will be exquisitely poetic. . . .

By the time this 'working up' period is complete and it is time to start rehearsals, a few directors may have mapped out every move (both of those of the actors and those of the cameras). Others start rehearsals with a more open mind. One or two start with a terrifyingly empty mind. The first are playing it safe. They are also limiting invention and restricting expression. Once it says in the script, 'CAMERA 2, CU JANE AT SINK', that is the way it is likely to remain. Those who come totally undecided undermine the confidence of the cast and annoy the technicians. They are also prone to overrun their schedules. The wise ones wait until they are well into the rehearsal period before finalising the camera script, and that rehearsal period begins either in a rehearsal room somewhere in the production company's building, or more likely in a distant church hall hired for the purpose.

At the first rehearsal, the director will usually say a little about the play and then ask the actors to risk a first read-through.

- 2 -

(ON CAM 3)

CROMWELL: Dear God in Heaven,
who searcheth our hearts and
knoweth all things that lie
buried in all men, You only are
worthy to be feared and trusted
and Your appearance patiently
waited upon. You will not fail
your people.

(CAMERA ON HIS FACE.
HE IS STRAINING,
FIGHTING TO REACH OUT
TO GOD)

/2 into 'A'/

Dear God, guide me in this thing
you have put upon me, Lord.
Dear God I am beset with fleshy
reasoning. Help me to recover
your Presence that has withdrawn
from me these three months ...
Dear God give me some sign, that
I can speak as in Your name to
this man ... Help me to accomplish
that work which will be for
the good of this Kingdom and all
its people ...

(FADE VOICE)

6.   2 A   /
      LS Charles   / 3C, 2A, 2B 4B/
      with dogs   /Fish   A2 /

      Hold his
      rise and   2. INT. THE KING'S PRIVATE APARTMENT.
      move L.

                          (CAMERA ON CHARLES'
                          ANGRY FACE. HE IS
                          RINGING HIS SILVER
                          BELL, IMPATIENTLY, FOR
                          HIS ATTENLANT, THOMAS
7.   4 B   HERBERT.
      MS entrance
      Let Herbert in   HERBERT RUSHES IN AND
                          BOWS TO THE KING)
8.   2 A   ON LOOK Row : ?
      2-S Herbert/
      Charles   HERBERT: Sir?

                          CHARLES: Sir, I have been
                          ringing that bell these five
9.   4 B   minutes!/
      MCU Herbert

      (CAM 2 NEXT)   - 2 -

A page of the camera script for Cecil P. Taylor's play *Charles and Cromwell*. For an
explanation of the terms and abbreviations, see pp. 135 and 162.

6.
The Cast

If you were to judge by the popular press, television is made entirely by the people who appear on the screen, be they presenters and interviewers or actors. It is their foibles, private lives and indiscretions that make the tabloid headlines, just as the writing-out of a leading character from a soap opera catches far more attention that does the sacking of a scriptwriter or director. When a new drama series is being launched on ITV, the programme journal *TV Times* (and much of the other publicity) is more likely to centre on the stars than on the author. There is nothing surprising about this. The public naturally identifies with those people whom they actually see as being involved in a production; and actors do tend to be more glamorous and interesting than sound engineers, at least so far as the public image has it.

What is surprising is that, in return, actors have so little influence on what appears on the screen. Even the actor who is known to question every note he gets from a theatrical director will be docile and obedient in the studio or when filming, as David Hare has pointed out:

> If an actor is asked to move quicker in the theatre, he will at once ask why. He will need to have a good reason in his head in order to be able to justify his speed every night. And if the reason is not good, his performance will deteriorate. But on film he will obey without asking, for he knows the basic truth of film making, that only the director can see. Only the director knows how the images are to be composed, more important, only he knows how they are to fit together, and because every image must finally pass through this single brain, the actor accepts that his job is to serve, on trust.[1]

Put in simplistic terms, a stage production is created by the dramatist, director and actors. In the television play, the ruling triumvirate is producer, director and writer. So what is the actor's contribution to television drama?

Often, that contribution is undervalued even within the production house. You need only ask an actor to discover the truth of this. Seriously, one must admit that there are many directors (especially those who have not worked in the theatre) who treat actors as not much more than mobile props, to be ignored when they are in the right place and cursed when in the wrong one. No wonder actors like what they call 'an actors' director', by which they mean one who understands their problems and needs.

To a certain extent, those problems and needs are the same as the ones faced by an actor on stage. They include the need to grasp an understanding of the play, the motivation of their own character and that character's relationship to the others in the play, together with all the emotional problems inherent in the business of rehearsing and performing. It is not, however, within the scope of this book to analyse the craft of acting in general terms (any more than it is to analyse the skills required by the theatrical director). What we are concerned with here are the specific requirements of television drama.

The first point to appreciate is that actors receive little training in acting for television. A few of course enter the profession without any training at all, but even those who attend what are significantly often known as 'stage schools' may have had only perfunctory instruction in working to the camera and microphone. Television cameras, lighting, sound and the recording equipment are expensive and few schools can afford to maintain an adequately equipped television drama studio. Short courses arranged in television training-establishments (be they commercial institutions or departments within educational establishments) are often superficial and fail to combine successfully both television and drama skills in one course. As a result, some actors pride themselves on their ignorance of the technicalities of the medium. 'No good asking me, darling, I don't know one end of a camera from the other. I just get on with my job, and let them do theirs.'

Mercifully there are those who have taken the trouble to

understand and master the demands and the potential of the medium. Shaun Sutton (who has been an actor, director and producer) has described how the television actor can and must use the hardware:

> As rehearsals progress, he will want to know where the camera is during his speeches, and how close his image will be. He must play to that camera, though not directly, as he would to an audience, if on a very different level. Tell him he is in close-up and he will adjust voice and pitch; if in long shot, pin high to the viewer, he knows he can open out a bit (at the same time wanting to know why he is *not* in close shot). But neither camera nor microphone will accept theatrical bravura. Acting in television is an intimate matter.
>
> Good acting is a blessed balance between natural talent, thought, instinct and technique. Cameras and microphones have sharp eyes and ears, registering the most fleeting expression, the smallest whisper. The television actor must know how to use both.[2]

Writing in the *Radio Times*, the theatre critic Michael Billington noted how such a gifted television actor as Ian Holm can use the camera:

> What is fascinating about Ian Holm's performance is his incessant watchfulness. I recalled a shot in the television adaptation of Iris Murdoch's *The Bell* when the camera panned across a group of people at prayer and picked up the tiniest flicker of lust as it passed his face.[3]

Many actors begin work in television by seeking an audition at the BBC. If they win one, they will have an interview and be asked to perform briefly in front of the cameras with a director watching on a monitor screen. The audition may or may not be taped. Sometimes particular actors are invited to audition for particular parts and will be seen by the director of the play being cast. Auditions are rare in independent television companies, where casting-directors use their knowledge of work actors have done to cast new productions. Nobody would claim it is easy for a young actor to get started in television, but once that first foothold has been gained then actors can trade on work done to catch and please the eye of those who have that prize of 'work' within their gift. These days more and more actors keep video tapes of their performances in order to be able to show directors or casting-directors their dazzlingly successful interpretations of Man in Pub, Lady in Bus Queue or Servant (non-speaking) the moment there is a chance they might just get the infinitely more demanding part of Truculent Man in Pub, Weary Lady in Bus Queue or even Servant (speaking).

Rehearsal for a television play is not like rehearsal time in the theatre. The latter is a comparatively leisurely process with a script being unpicked, worked over, put together again; with characterisations being slowly built, with the pace and rhythms being developed until the production has a life of its own and is strong enough to survive a first night and possibly a lengthy run. It is rather like cultivating a precious plant which must burst into bloom every evening at half past seven for as long as it lives. In television the process is speeded up. So long as each scene looks right the moment it is caught by the camera, that is sufficient.

Suppose it is a studio-based production. The first read-through may be followed by discussion with the writer. There will certainly be time for discussion and questions between cast and director. Then comes the serious business of learning lines and of getting the script off the page. In the rehearsal room, coloured sticky tape on the floor indicates the size of the set. A chair represents a throne. In many ways these early days of rehearsal are quite similar to the same period in the life of a stage play; but, even more insistently than in the theatre, there are reminders that time is money. Even so, the formal 10 a.m. to 6 p.m. rehearsal day is broken up by tea breaks of union-agreed dimensions, and also (at varying stages in the rehearsal period) by days filming on location and by audio pre-recording sessions.

The latter will involve recording voice-only sequences in a sound studio. For example, it might be necessary to record what will become 'voice-over' narrative links or the 'thoughts' of a character. Later, this sound track will be dubbed on to the master tape, or played in during the actual recording of the visual action to which they relate.

For an actor used to the theatre, recording or filming on

location can be an unnerving process. In his autobiography, Sir John Gielgud has described his early experiences of working 'in public':

> We filmed in lower Manhattan on location, then a fairly new experience for me, where they took out one side of a taxi-cab, while the cameraman sat right in front of us on the floor, to photograph us as we drove along. It was a very hot day and we went round and round the fish-market, which smelt to high heaven. In the next scene I had to climb on to the roof of another taxi, still rather drunk, carrying a briefcase and umbrella and wearing a bowler hat and city suit, and harangue the crowd. We were shooting in a busy street opposite a girls' school, and all the girls were hanging out of the windows and screaming with laughter.[4]

In the same chapter, he describes the problem of 'waiting' – waiting until the light is correct for a particular shot, till intrusive noise has died down and until the equipment is ready:

> One must learn to be patient, waiting for hours between takes and set-ups . . . but at the same time one must be ready to snap into one's performance the moment one is needed, ignoring the inconsistencies of continuity. Sometimes only a look may be required, sometimes only a reaction to a speech from another character, sometimes quite a long speech or scene for a main long shot.

Where there is a good rapport between director and cast, the rehearsal period (on location and in the rehearsal room) can be fun. 'Actors' directors' love this part of the production and actors usually respond. They enjoy talking about roles, about ways of playing a scene, about subtle emphases, about *acting*. This is, to the actor, a familiar process, similar to the run up of any 'opening'.

If all has gone well, by now the cast will feel at home with the play, they know its shape, its climaxes and its pace. There may have been minor rewrites ('Wouldn't it be more natural if I said . . .'), there may have been disagreements, there may not be quite the same family atmosphere that is often found in a theatre, but there is some sort of team spirit. Then, just before the production moves into the studio, there is what is known as the 'Producer's run'. A typical such rehearsal has been described by the actor Clive Swift:

You've had two weeks' rehearsal for an hour's play. Towards the end of the second week the rehearsal room will be visited by the producer and his staff and a representative selection of technicians who are working on the show. They will know the script and will no doubt have had meetings with the director, agreeing on what can or can't be done. But this is the first time they've seen the piece in action. Atmosphere in the rehearsal room grows more tense that day. This is your first audience (and will be your last): that's what's so unnerving about people closely watching shows arranged for television. The director has thought how best it should be done in terms of cameras, machines that can capture nose flickers or make the angle of an ear most significant, and there you are faced (positively crowded out) by real live people, and people who are hard to impress (they've become immune to a great deal of what plays and actors can do!). It requires great self-control to do what the director expects you to do: part of oneself wants to 'entertain the folks'! You are confused. Who is your performance for? To whom are you offering it? The cameras.[5]

From now on, so it will seem to the actor, everything must serve the needs of the camera. No wonder the producer's run (where everyone is considering how it will look on camera, but where there are no cameras) is an unnatural happening.

After the producer's run, perhaps the very next day, the play moves into the studio. In a later chapter we shall consider all the various trades and activities that come together there during technical rehearsals and recording. Here it is relevant to note some of the pressures that weigh upon the actor, pressures which he gets little chance to vocalise, which disturb even the most experienced television actor and which stem from the many splendid little surprises which lie in wait for him.

First, there is the costume. During rehearsals measurements have been taken and there have been fittings. However, costumes have a way of developing and, although the actor knew there was going to be a cloak (indeed he had been rehearsing in one), he did not realise quite how heavy the real one would be; she knew that she was to be tightly corseted but not that tightly. . . . Usually the actor's costume awaits him or her in a dressing-room, possibly with a dresser in attendance. Dressers can be friendly, ignorant, flirtatious, even helpful. Besides actually assisting actors in and out of costumes and helping with any quick changes, dressers are responsible for washing, ironing and pressing costumes.

Next, the actor goes to Make-up. In the theatre, almost every actor applies his or her own make-up in a dressing-room. In television, there is a central make-up area under the direction of the make-up designer and her make-up artists. The actor dare not touch so much as a powder puff but lies back in a chair. At its best, the actor's time in make-up can be charmingly therapeutic. At its worst, it can be hot, uncomfortable and tiring. It too can spring surprises. The actress knew her nose was going to be built up, but quite so much as that? And that scar/blister/wart? Was it to be so obvious?

The actor is now ready to wait. And wait.

Waiting may be a solitary activity in the dressing-room. It may be undertaken in the studio while carpenters, electricians, props assistants and set dressers also stand around waiting while a lamp is moved, a carpet is tacked into place or a camera or microphone move is rehearsed.

This period gives the actor time to get either hot and flustered or cold and tense. There is also time to ponder on a table which has changed from the domestic kitchen table used in rehearsal to one that might support a medieval banquet. How will he or she be able to hand cups of tea round that? Occasionally, the actor catches a fleeting glimpse of the director as he scuttles back up the iron staircase into the control gallery, mouthing a 'Shan't be long', before disappearing out of sight for ever. No chance now for a word about the table, wart, nose or cloak.

Eventually rehearsals begin. Unlike the rehearsal room, you no longer enter an acting-area the moment you see your leading lady look downcast, moving tenderly to comfort her. You wait behind the scenery, out of sight, until the floor manager gives you a cue. Then there's a problem. Everything stops. Everyone but the cast is wearing tiny headsets which allow them to hear what is said in the control gallery, and to talk back to the gods upstairs. Silence. They're all listening. Then they all laugh. A cameraman says into his microphone, 'It wasn't that bad.' Everyone laughs again. Was that your performance? A technical fault? Desperately, the actor catches the eye of his only link with the world above, the floor manager (or production assistant – the terms vary from one production house to another). 'Was I . . . all right?' The floor manager puts a finger to his earpiece. 'Just a minute.' He listens to those above and then walks away. A minute later he's back.

'Look. You know that bit where you're sitting on the sofa, listening intently?'

'Yes. Was I . . . ?'

'You were fine. But as you listen, do you think you could lean right back, just so we can get a two-shot of them without getting you in camera? That'll be fine. Right back like that. Lovely. Just relax.'

Other problems surface. The actor discovers that there will be a break in his tempestuous argument with his girlfriend in order to allow Camera 2 time to get into a new position. In the next scene, the sofa won't be in the sitting-room. The viewer won't notice and it'll allow both Cameras 2 and 4 to get in close. The fact that it now seems a very different 'room' from what it was a moment ago is immaterial.

Eventually the technical problems are ironed out. No matter that what was once a fluent, exciting play is now a series of disconnected scenes, probably to be recorded out of sequence because it is 'easier' (i.e. easier for the crew, for the cameras, for everyone except the actors). There is no audience and little reaction from the technicians on the floor of the studio. How do you know if it is working? The actor is alone. Suddenly it is time to go for a 'take'. There are sighs of relief all round at the thought of 'getting something in the can'.

A scene is played. It breaks down half way through.

Back to the top.

Play it again. It works. The actor is relieved, knowing inwardly that he was right, even brilliant. Wait. Everyone is listening on their headsets. 'What!' There was the shadow of a microphone boom on someone's face. Start again. This time the actor is less than good. He did nothing wrong, it was just, well, not so good. He waits, expecting to be asked to do it again. Everyone smiles. No, it was fine. No shadows, no problems.

'But I could do it better –'

'No, honestly. It's OK. We must press on. . . .'

Gradually, progress is made, scene by scene. There are terrible delays because a radio microphone starts playing up, because a camera goes 'on the blink' or because a detail of someone's costume or a surface of a table starts to 'flare' or reflect in the lights. Suddenly it is five to six. If recording goes on after six o'clock, there will be enormous overtime bills to be paid to every technician. The last scene takes three and a half minutes to play.

'We'll go for a take, straight off.'

Everyone rushes into position.

'But do I . . . . Where do I put –'

'It's all right.'

Four minutes to six. Tension.

Tape is rolling.

'On a cue.'

And then, after a day of waiting for everyone else, the actor finally receives a helpful comment.

'Try not to fluff, won't you?'

It is not all that different out filming, as Sir John Gielgud has recorded:

> In films, once you decide on your performance and have created it broadly in a key scene taken in long shot, you must be prepared to repeat it in correctly similar detail in the closeups and two-shots which complete the photographing of the whole scene. People keep coming up, maddeningly, and saying, 'You must put your hand to your haversack on this line', or, 'You touched your tie.' You did those things

not knowing you did them, so that when you are then reminded of them for a week, you suddenly become frighteningly sick of the scene; it is a boring repetition of something you would rather do in a different way each time. The continuity girl is continually at your elbow, reminding you of your exact movements and gestures when the main scene was shot, yet you may also have to move your head or hands to a slightly different angle to satisfy the lighting or the camera or feed your partner from behind the camera with lines from the scene that he or she is reacting to in close-up. Wardrobe assistants and hairdressers brush you down or spruce you up, powder and dry your face just before you start to act. A babel of conversation and argument is suddenly quelled and an unnatural deadly silence falls as the fatal three bells are rung and the clapperboard is snapped jauntily within an inch of your face. Worst of all, you know that whatever you do, once accepted by the director, is there forever. No chance to develop or improve at a subsequent performance or bring greater subtlety to bear on your original conception.[6]

Television drama does of course also bring rewards to actors. It can bring success and fame, which some actors relish for their own sake. How they like the fun of being recognised, of special attention in a restaurant, and of feeling that everyone knows them and what they do. Wise actors know that the real value of success on television lies in the likelihood of it bringing more work, both on television and on stage. Wise actors also know the drawbacks of fame: the loss of privacy, the intrusion of the public on private occasions, and the need constantly to maintain a public image.

Television drama also brings money. Series and serials bring more money. As Jean Marsh (who played the houseparlour maid, Rose, in *Upstairs, Downstairs*) has said, 'Before the series, I'd never lived in more than two rooms. Then along came Rose and I was able to put down a deposit and raise a mortgage.'

A part in a long-running serial also brings security, regular hours and a removal of the actor's constant need to look for work. However, it can lead to the acquisition of a fixed identity in the minds of the public and casting-directors. Once a window cleaner, always a window cleaner. Consequently being written out of a serial or the ending of a serial presents special problems to the actor. The traditional advice is 'Get back into the theatre until the viewers remember you can do other things.' But there are more positive aspects to such a parting. It means a release from the weekly chore of learning new lines and it means the chance to play a variety of roles again, either in the theatre or (despite all the problems) back in the television studios once again.

7.
Design

While the actual rehearsal period leading up to the recording of a play may be, say, three weeks, the design teams will have become involved much earlier. For example, the costume designer will have joined a major Shakespearean production team at least twelve weeks before recording and will (according to Maggie McPherson, head of the BBC's Costume Department) 'work more than full time for those twelve weeks'.

Costume is only one of several branches of a television design group. The main sections are scenic design, costume, lighting, make-up, special effects and graphics. We shall consider the role of lighting in television drama (and also the contributions made by the sound department) in the next two chapters. In this chapter we shall look at each of the other sections in turn. First it is relevant to note the planning-meetings that precede the creative work of each section. A typical sequence was outlined by Richard Lewin (one-time head of the BBC Television Design Group) in the *BBC Handbook* for 1968:

> The director holds a briefing meeting attended by the scenic and costume designers and the technical manager responsible for lighting. They will, by then, all have read the script and will be briefed on the mood, the action and the number of costume changes required in the play. At this time references are looked up, researches got under way and film locations found. Visuals of the key shots will be drawn and a rough studio plan worked out to show all the settings and likely camera positions.

This meeting is followed by the all-important co-ordination meeting which will also include the make-up specialist, the sound supervisor and, if he is involved in the programme, the effects designer. The costume designer now presents his drawings and sample fabrics and the scenic designer, his plans and sketches, so that agreement can be reached all round on the shape and overall colour treatment of the play. Following on this agreement, the director will consult with the graphic designer on the opening and closing titles for the programme.[1]

Following further researches, there are more consultations. Technical staff report on the feasibility of the planned sets and other designs, and there is a final co-ordination meeting in which the entire creative team discusses and agrees all the plans, changes and amendments. Following this finalisation of planning, each department can begin work: work that involves trades as diverse as carpenters and wigmakers, upholsterers and armourers, sculptors and florists, signwriters and machinists.

Scenic Design

Suppose a scene of a play takes place within a Victorian sitting-room. It is no good designing and building a Victorian sitting-room as realistically as possible. It will prove impossible to light, there will be no room for the cameras to move about in and, most importantly, it will not be a convincing Victorian sitting-room when viewed on a small screen. It must be designed for television.

Television scenery is known by various names: the set or setting, the staging, or décor. It may represent a never-never land of make-believe or be a realistic setting which is apparently true to history and geography; and, whether the scenic designer is creating a supposedly accurate Roman forum, a contemporary hospital ward or a centre of high technology on an imaginary planet in the thirtieth century AD, his or her aim must be the same. It is to create an illusion, an illusion that this is a real place at a particular moment in time. It must additionally be a setting in which actors can be comfortable: they must seem to belong there. It must also be usable by the machinery of television. It must take into account the qualities of a camera lens. (When using a wide-angle lens, a camera can exaggerate distance; a narrow-angle lens contracts space and depth. It may be possible to use these qualities creatively or the scenic designer may use unreal proportions and perspectives to counter them.) The set must have suitable sound acoustics so that, for example, there is no echo effect in what is meant to be a well-furnished lounge. More importantly, it must not exceed the budget.

The scenic designer (or designer, as he or she is usually known) must therefore be both an artist and a scientist, a historian and an accountant; someone who knows about seventeenth-century royal palaces, the effect of light on different surfaces and the best ways of saving money without it showing. He or she must have the imagination to create a new world for *Dr Who* and the patience to recreate the interior of a police station so as to convince every watching desk sergeant.

The designer is responsible not only for settings constructed for studio use. On location work, he or she is responsible for altering the stately home, urban street or village green to suit the production. This may mean adding extra street furniture (such as a horse trough, if the script requires it) or even extra battlements, towers and statues. It may mean removing, hiding or disguising features (such as telegraph poles, bus-stop signs and modern extensions to historic properties). Tons of sand may be needed to cover double yellow lines in the main street and shop names will have to be altered. Even modern plays dictate changes in reality. It may, for example, be imperative that there be a launderette opposite the café in which the corpse is found.

Where a mixture of location and studio work is combined in one production, then the designer is responsible for continuity. If we see the outside of a hotel on location and its interior in the studio, then not only must obvious things be right, such as the windows remaining a constant shape and size, but when the front door opens it must be the same colour in both settings and look the same shade in natural light and in studio lighting.

Following initial planning-meetings (in which such matters as the amount of location and studio work will have been settled), the designer has to come up with basic ideas that suit the script and the director's interpretation. For both historical and contemporary plays this will involve a period of research. No designer is keen to have eagle-eyed viewers writing to the *Radio Times* about anachronisms. For more fantastical productions this period is all the more exciting. For example, the BBC Television Shakespeare production of *The Tempest* was particularly striking and innovative. This magical play takes place on an island which must itself be realistic. The director John Gorrie and designer Paul Joel settled on Renaissance Italy as the period of the production.

> The reference material used for the sets was primarily the Doré illustrations for *The Divine Comedy:* 'I remember', says Gorrie, 'looking through *Paradise Lost* when I was at school, and seeing the crags and rocks of the Doré illustrations, and that's what I wanted.' *The Divine Comedy* proved to have more potential source material than *Paradise Lost* and that is what set designer Paul Joel ended up using, along with photographs of actual cliffs, islands and rock formations. For Prospero's cave, says the director, 'I didn't want a mini-cave: I wanted a great cleft in the rocks, not unlike the sort of thing you find in Yorkshire. I vaguely remembered seeing a photograph of the sort of cave I had in mind, and Paul came up with a book of photographs which had the actual photograph in it.'
> Fundamentally what the play needed was a high cliff face, an olive grove and a dust-bowl beach – or at least an area that's absolutely bare and barren: after all, Trinculo says, 'Here's neither bush nor shrub to bear off any weather at all.'[2]

Obviously the designer cannot simply move from ideas to an experimental building-session in the studio. He or she works instead with plans and models. Always available to a designer are printed outline plans of the studio in which the recording will take place. On these are marked such immovables as studio doorways, staircases, camera plugging-points, electricity- and water-supply points, scenery hoists and fire exits.

Around these the designer can plan the distribution of the different sets that he or she dreams up. For *The Tempest*,

> Joel, to accommodate all three areas and give as much fluidity and perspective as possible, created a circular set, one area blending into another all the way round the circumference of the large Studio 1 at Television Centre, with cameras and technicians working from the centre.

Designers also prepare models of their intended sets. These allow everyone working on a production to get a clearer idea of its appearance, its three-dimensional qualities and its potential:

> 'If you can shoot from one set into another you get more room, greater perspective and greater depth', points out Gorrie. In his office Paul Joel has three models of the set, all similar, though the differences turn out to be crucial – at least between the first two models. 'I took the first model down to our estimator and he said, "You can't afford that!" so it had to be rationalised. Looking at it again I felt we didn't really require quite so much irregularity, and rationalising it I think produced a better result.' The actual end-product, I remark, looks more like the Doré inspiration than the first model, which has a rather more Gothic quality. He agrees and points out that it was those overhangs and projecting shapes which accounted for the daunting estimate on Model One.

All the time, the designer must bear in mind the restrictions of the budget and refer to the production's estimator. He must not only cost the materials the set will consume; also to be kept in mind are the man hours it will take to construct, the costs of transportation and storage and the restrictions caused by studio schedules. Some economies can be borne in mind from the earliest stages, especially if a director is prepared to commit himself to particular shots. For example, suppose there is a scene in an office. If the director is prepared to say that we shall never see the room from its occupant's point of view but always look at him sitting behind his desk, then the designer need only plan the two walls behind the desk. Other directors will not accept this sort of limitation and may not settle for specific camera angles until the production is in the studio. Here the designer must create a 'complete' set and subsequently find himself 'offering' particular movements or shorts to the director because they look well on the screen. (Strictly speaking, no set is complete. The 'fourth wall' is almost always missing.)

The basic rule for every designer must be, 'If we're not going to see it, don't build it.' However, this means very careful planning and the need to keep in mind possible changes in camera angles in all three dimensions, including elevation. It is no good building only the trunk and lower branches of a tree if a shot from a low angle will reveal its higher branches. Also to be kept in mind is the question of which sets will be seen in close-up as well as in long shots. All the time, the design must suggest to the viewer that the rest of the room, street or forest is there if only it could be seen. That said, it is easy to cheat. Significant foreground details (e.g. the parapet of a bridge) can suggest far more than they actually show (especially with the help of a wind machine and sound effects). Painted scenery or photographic enlargements can be cheated into three-dimensional sets by merging their lower edges with a painted studio floor and a sense of distance achieved by placing scenic items (e.g. archways or bushes) on different planes between camera and backgrounds. Similarly it is possible to cheat perspective by placing larger furniture near the camera and smaller items further away, so suggesting spaciousness.

Studio space is always at a premium. Many a designer has spent hours with pieces of paper, each a scaled-down representation of a particular set, shunting them around a studio plan in the vain hope that in one arrangement they will all fit into the studio. An added problem will be caused by any sequence of scenes that are to be shot without a break between them. Can actors get from one set to another quickly enough? More importantly, can cameras get from one to another without their cables becoming entwined?

Over the years a number of standard ploys have come into use to resolve some of the problems. A 'pack' of sets can be built. Removing the one nearest the camera reveals another location behind it. Hinged flats can be opened up to reveal another one on the reverse of the first. A small set can be built inside a larger one for a particular scene and removed when it is no longer required, or it can be built on a flat truck and wheeled into the studio just for the scenes in which it is needed.

The designer must always remember, as must everyone else, the needs of a camera. Cameramen (and the director) want a variety of shots in each scene. It is no good building a corridor in which a camera can do no more than peep from one end, nor is it any good building a claustrophobic set (even if the script specifies it) if there is no room for the camera. As is so often the case in television, it is possible to cheat. Cameras can look through windows (provided another camera is not looking out through that window). Special peepholes can be constructed, or bookcases can be mounted on wheels so that they can slide aside. Curtains can be moved to allow camera access and see-through mirrors can offer other positions. Bushes, ornamental screens and overlapping sections of a wall can all hide a camera as well.

The tone and colour of each element of the set are also important. Very bright areas will result in too much light reaching the camera. There may be distracting reflections or a loss of detail (e.g. the camera may not see pencil writing on a very white page). Over-dark areas will cause their own problems, such as murkiness or even electronic interference. Colours can be too bright and look simply brash or vulgar. Designers therefore avoid bright reds and blues and settle for pastel and muddy colours. Also to be taken into account is the set's appearance on a monochrome (i.e. black-and-white) receiver. Bright blue sky can look boringly overcast and two contrasting colours can reduce to precisely the same shade of grey.

Further restrictions are caused by safety requirements, as Gerald Millerson summarises in his very practical manual on television staging:

Safety considerations are a principal concern in all staging. The aspects needing care are diverse: firm, stable construction; suitable weight distribution and loading; fireproofed scenery and dressings; no unguarded stairs or high points; non-slip floor surfaces; no precariously balanced furniture or properties; no sharp-edged or spiked projections; no easily shattered materials (e.g. glass windows); no materials liable to explode or give off noxious fumes; no hazards of fire, gas, water, steam. . . . The list is long, so long that for network studios the required precautions fill substantial safety manuals. But even workers in small studios would do well to be wary of potential dangers.[3]

Of course some designers, such as those working on long-running serials, have had most of their problems solved for them over the years. Everyone knows what the Rover's Return looks like: it is just a matter of keeping it up to date. Yet even *Coronation Street* has its problems. Originally outdoor scenes were recorded on location in Salford. Then an outdoor set was built on Granada TV property in 1968. However, this could only be of two-thirds scale and camera angles had to be selected so as to make it appear full-scale on the screen. A new set has been built more recently, using old bricks and slates from nearby demolition sites to maintain a period finish. Most viewers probably failed to detect the change, but those working on it noticed many a new freedom.

Whether it is the comparatively minor requirements of a serial or an original venture such as a single play, the designer will eventually be able to produce the final studio plans. These are copied. The director needs a number on which to work out moves (of cast and cameras) and those who will create the sets need theirs. The number of people required to create a complex series of sets is impressive, as can be seen from Figure 1, which summarises the design process from initiation to destruction.

Once construction is under way the designer is less immediately involved, although there will be frequent consultation meetings between him and the various departments charged with the creation of the different components of the set, over such matters as the texture of surfaces, whether a particular set needs smartening up or 'dressing down' and whether modifications are needed to cheat the eye of the camera.

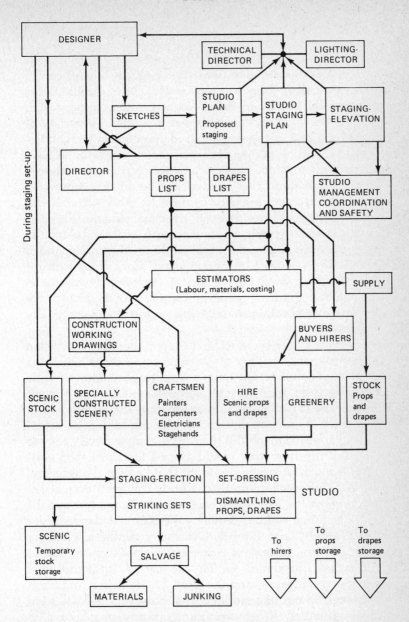

FIGURE 1   The design process

Source: Gerald Millerson, *Basic TV Staging*, 2nd edn (London and Boston, Mass.: Focal Press, 1982) p. 13.

The day (or night) before studio rehearsals and recordings begin, the designer will oversee the erection of the set in the studio. Much earlier he or she will have decided on the various floor surfaces that are to be used. These will be created before or (more usually) after the erection of the sets. Studio floors are normally made of hard-wearing, non-slippery lino stretched on wood. Scenic artists can simulate a variety of surfaces on these, using water-based paint to suggest cobblestones, slabs, tiles, planks or carpets. Most large studios have floor-painting machines which can apply certain set patterns. (After a production, the 'surface' can be quickly removed.) Standard substances are used to simulate other surfaces and to decorate painted ones. For soil, the usual substitute is peat. Sawdust is used to represent sand or earth (real sand being too abrasive for use in a studio), and white sawdust or expanded polystyrene granules can imitate snow. Cork chips look remarkably like gravel. Note that it is far more convenient in television to use 'silent' gravel and to add sound effects at the right sound level rather than coping with real and erratically noisy gravel.

Once erected, the set must be dressed under the supervision of the designer, designer's assistant or someone with this special responsibility. Curtains are put up at windows (white net having been dyed grey to look used and also to prevent glare on camera), chairs placed at pre-arranged positions and rooms made to look as though they belong to the characters who are supposed to inhabit them. It is comparatively easy to create a sitting-room that would grace a furniture-shop window. It is much harder to create one that looks as though, say, a house-proud mother and three untidy children have battled in it for five years. Props are checked and arranged around the set or where they will be needed by the actors, and greenery is finally brought onto the set. Obviously synthetic greenery (plastic flowers, fibreglass tree trunks, plastic grass, and so on) can be introduced earlier, as can dead items (real branches, dead leaves, and the like). Living plants and fresh cut flowers do not like studio lights, however, and will need constant attention. When everything is ready, people rush up to the designer from all directions and say, 'Congratulations, marvellous, but do you think we could just re-spray/paint/move/change. . . .'

Costume Design

In the mid seventies, BBC Television made a serial dramatisation of Tolstoy's novel, *Anna Karenina*. Nicola Pagett played Anna and, in the course of nine hours of television, had thirty-four costume changes. In one scene of this nineteenth-century story, a hundred people were seen skating (on nineteenth-century ice-skates). That scene was recorded on location in Budapest. Every week of the year, scores of actors appear on screen as everything from nurses, army officers and politicians to tramps, teachers and monsters from outer space. All must be costumed, accurately and convincingly. It is the responsibility of the costume designer to hire, make or buy those costumes and to have them in the right place at the right time.

Costume designers have usually been to art school and are likely to have a degree in theatre costume, fashion or some aspect of the history of art or design. They may have worked in the theatre, as a costumier or in the 'rag trade'. They tend to enter television as costume-design assistants and learn the specific requirements of the medium 'on the job', and quickly. In the BBC, they are members of the staff and work on a variety of programmes. Having designed a classic serial, they might next work on a situation comedy or a light-entertainment show. The 'gems' for a costume designer are shows where he or she can actually design costumes as opposed to 'merely' get them right. Thus a Shakespeare or a good *Dr Who* serial is a more exciting challenge than, say, a costume drama.

The costume designer works to the director. Some directors have strong ideas about costume, others 'haven't got a clue', to quote one designer. As we have seen earlier, the costume designer is involved in planning-meetings and must liaise with the scenic designer, but the costume designer does not work to the designer's orders. 'Definitely not' according to Maggie McPherson, BBC's head of costume. The relationship between the two designers can be splendidly harmonious, although it must be admitted that, when ideas or preferred colours and styles are found to clash, there can be conflict. Indeed the story is told of a famous punch-up on a Shakespeare.

When planning costumes, the designer must also take into account lighting and technical requirements and therefore have meetings with the lighting-supervisor and technical-operations manager. It is no good selecting brilliant white robes for a group of angels if they will 'flare' in the studio lights. Also to be avoided are very bright reds and blues, as are sharp contrasts of black and white. Much more effective are sludge colours, greens and beiges or contrasts of dark grey and cream.

Clearly enough, the costume designer must be familiar with the script. She will also be desperate for further information. 'How are you going to interpret this role? Will she be youngish or middle-aged? Is he going to be seen in close-up? How many are in the army? Are they going to get muddy?' Even more importantly, 'Can I have the cast list?' The answer to the last question is almost invariably, 'Not yet.' It seems one of those inevitable facts of television production that the costume designer must start work long before the cast is finalised.

Once designs have been agreed there comes the task of actually finding or making the costumes. Most are hired in order to keep within the budget. 'Save your money for the principals, especially the females', is the working-rule of many a designer. Some costumes have to be bought. The costume designer will go shopping, perhaps in London's Portobello Road market on the lookout for the fashions of the 1950s or even in Savile Row to please a star who can play an aristocrat only in the best of suits. Many costumes have to be made specially and then the designer will give a very clear brief to the freelance out-workers who specialise in making costumes for television.

Designers need also to keep in close touch with contemporary fashion. For example, when dressing *Grange Hill* (the BBC's serial set in a London comprehensive school), the designer must know just what length of skirt would be right for a certain girl or how that boy would wear his tie. In some ways, the police, services and medical staff are easy: you just try to get it right, but rest assured that viewers will notice the incorrect button arrangement, the wrong shade of green in a tunic or the clergyman in unseasonable vestments. Viewers also have excellent memories about the way characters have dressed in earlier episodes of a serial which the designer may never have seen.

The order in which the various scenes are to be recorded, as well as their locations, must be kept in mind. Location work is, so far as costumes are concerned, a dirtier occupation than studio work. The designer may therefore have to get a costume back to pristine freshness for a studio scene that is to be recorded after a location one but which appears earlier in the play. Sometimes two sets of the same costume (one clean, one 'dirty') will be required.

During rehearsal and filming or recording, the director may frequently consult the costume designer about etiquette, expecting her to know when eighteenth-century ladies kept their hats on and when they took them off, what ladies did with their gloves in the next century, who would stand up when a minister of the crown came into a room and when a Victorian parlour maid would curtsey. It is a job with its chores: wasting forty-eight hours trying to track down a star actor in order to measure his shoulders, being patient with testy actors and hanging around for hours during filming for little apparent purpose. The main reward is the personal satisfaction of knowing that you have 'got it right'. Sometimes other people notice this as well. Occasionally they say so.

Make-up

Television make-up is more than the fashion make-up used in daily life. It is also more than cosmetic make-up to hide spots, blotches and wrinkles from the camera's penetrating gaze. It is an art at the service of director and designers, ready to transform an actor into a character. It is also a technique which serves to make faces (and bodies) appear on screen as they are intended to. This may mean applying powder or eau-de-Cologne to stop perspiration; it may be the application of imitation sweat for a jungle scene.

Make-up artists will have studied art and obtained relevant City and Guilds diplomas. They are also skilled hairdressers. Beginning as trainees, they graduate to the rank of make-up assistant, then to make-up artist and on to make-up supervisor or designer.

Much of their work is fairly routine: the applying of a base to an actor's face to stop it appearing deathly white in the studio lights, with a little addition of colour to the cheeks and attention to the eyes. It can also involve the fitting of wigs (hairy or bald) which will have been made to order in advance, ageing a face, perhaps adding an artificial double chin – and making sure that no joins are visible to the camera. Ageing may mean 'changing' the face of an actor for the one production or it may have to indicate a 'slow' process over eight episodes of a serial.

Occasionally unnatural make-up must be designed for aliens, ghosts and monsters; and make-up departments also counterfeit the effects of battles, accidents, crashes and woundings.

On location, the make-up team may be able to use a convenient room in the hotel, castle or holiday camp in which recording or filming is taking place. If it is in a more isolated location then a caravan must be hired and towed as near to the location as possible.

In a studio complex, there will be a make-up suite near the studio in which the production is being recorded. Make-up rooms are usually havens of peace and gossip.

Special Effects

There is an entire science of special effects required by (and created for) television drama. Some are 'trick' props, some special visual effects that can be created physically on location or in a studio and some electronics.

The tools of the trade of the special-effects designer range from polystyrene, plaster of Paris and glass fibre to mirrors, explosives and models. He can also use flame forks (not unlike a multi-pronged gas poker), a cobweb gun (a small portable electric fan which sprays a latex solution) and such old stand-bys of the theatre as wind machines, dry-ice generators (to create mist) and bottles made of wax which can be broken on the heads of valuable actors. The special-effects designer knows how to blend models with life-size scenes. For example, he can match model ships on a model pond with a short length of a ship's deck rail so that the viewer believes he is seeing a naval battle from Nelson's flagship. He knows too about controlled (and safe) explosions, how to make bullets appear to go through doors and people, about trick knives and swords, and about ways of making swamps out of Fuller's earth and water. Dry ice thrown into this mixture makes it bubble exotically. The special-effects designer is usually responsible whenever water is brought into the studio. (In fact spectacular floods and cascades are usually recorded out of the studio, but shallow pools can be constructed in a studio to simulate a lake or pond.)

One electronic or video effect has been used to increasing advantage over the last ten years or so. In Independent Television companies it is known as Chroma Key and within the BBC as Colour Separation Overlay (or, with that organisation's delight in initials, CSO).

Basically this consists of placing one picture on top of another. This of course can be done quite easily without any special equipment, but then every element of each picture would be seen. For example, if one picture was of a person and the other of a wall, we should see the wall 'through' the person. CSO or Chroma Key stops this 'see-through' effect.

Let us suppose a play needs the effect of a person flying. One camera shows an area of sky. The second shot needs more careful planning. The background to the actor must be a plain colour (usually blue). The wires suspending him in space must be of the same colour. Care must then be taken to see that that tone of blue does not occur anywhere else in his picture. The 'brain' of the CSO or Chroma Key is a switching-unit. This is then programmed to the key colour. One picture is then superimposed precisely on top of the other. Wherever the switching-unit reads the specified colour in the second picture (of the actor), it inserts that area of the first picture. Consequently as the actor makes swimming (or 'flying') movements, all remaining areas of the picture frame around him will be filled with sky.

There are problems. The background must be constant and the actor in the foreground may become fringed with an intrusive colour. Nevertheless CSO has been used imaginatively in various stylised productions, such as the BBC's 1976 production of the Chester medieval mystery plays and in the more recent dramatisation of Voltaire's *Candide*. It has also come into its own in surrealistic scenes in *Dr Who* and *Blake's Seven*.

Graphics

Graphic-design departments have been, and continue to be, responsible for all printing and lettering connected with a production. Under their aegis come such things as the fascias for shops seen in plays, mocked-up newspapers and ancient scrolls. Graphics may be responsible for creating an imaginary company's 'image'. Perhaps a building-society figures prominently (and unfavourably) in a play. It will be impossible to refer to a real one so an imaginary one must be invented. Graphics must supply a logo, letterheads, passbooks. . . .

Graphics are also responsible for title sequences and closing credits. These are not merely informative. They contribute to the overall design of the play and, together with title music, are instrumental in communicating the mood and themes of the coming production. In the case of serials they can help to trigger accustomed responses and audience loyalty. Over the years, television has borrowed the cinema's penchant for elaborate, witty or symbolic title sequences.

The simplest form of titles is a series of still images combining, say, a picture or design with a title or credit (i.e. the author's name). These are known as captions. Designed and created by graphics, they are mounted on card and can be placed in front of the cameras on the studio floor. Camera 1 can 'read' the first, third and fifth captions, while Camera 2 takes the intervening ones. Caption cards can be changed manually when not in shot. It is usual to use a roller caption at the end of a production. All the credits are listed in order on a long roll of black paper which is then wound vertically or horizontally past a camera. Either still or roller captions can be superimposed on another picture.

Computer graphics are now rapidly replacing such methods. Computers can generate titles and credits almost as quickly as they can be typed. They are then superimposed on the screen, without the use of a camera. The most immediate use of this was in news and current affairs programmes, but its use has spread to other forms of production, particularly as devices have come onto the market which allow for three-dimensional lettering, the use of colour and greater clarity.

There is, for example, a machine called the Paint Box, made by Quantel Ltd. Using an electronic stylus, the graphics artist can 'paint' on an electronic canvas, while watching the picture grow on the screen. Paint Box has its equivalent of a palette in which colours can be mixed, together with a keyboard and a picture store. Paint Box can achieve what an art studio can, but in a twentieth of the time. Also being developed are computers which generate apparently three-dimensional objects onto the screen. Though still very stylised, they have considerable application in the making of advertisements and cartoons. They are bound to be of increasing use in drama, especially when stylisation is called for (e.g. in science fiction). Graphics promises to be a growth area within the design group.

8.

On Location

As we noted in the first chapter of this book, location filming has its many champions. So too, to a lesser extent, does location video recording. Both camps of enthusiasts feel that it is only out of the confines of the studio that the best television dramas can be made. Moreover, it is not only the makers of plays or films that hanker after the great outdoors. Viewers seem increasingly hungry for realistic, fast-moving and action-packed dramas or for visual feasts filmed or recorded on varied and exotic locations. Indeed, one theory has it that (with the exception of some serials) the studio play no longer has mass appeal.

So much for the desire and the demand. What are the practicalities of making drama on location? Obviously they vary according to the size of the operation in question: whether it is a matter of filming a major epic or just a few short scenes to be cut into a studio production, whether it is a full-size outside broadcast or only a lightweight unit recording part of a play on tape. Whatever the case, the operation must begin in the same way.

Planning

Any television drama is expensive. Location work is fiendishly so, and planning must take place to see that it is conducted as economically as possible. Travel needs to be kept to a minimum, which will almost certainly mean working on scenes out of their natural order. A whole variety of factors must be taken into account when choosing locations. Will it be

cheaper to wait for a sunny day in Southport's sandhills or
actually to go to the Sahara? Is there a suitable hotel at which
cast and crew can stay? Is there another indoor location
nearby which can be used for indoor scenes if bad weather
should delay use of the outdoor location? Have the owners of
the property (or the police or local authority) given permission
for filming or taping?

Once any play moves into rehearsal and production, the
production or 'unit' acquires a production assistant (BBC) or
floor manager (ITV). This vital person, along with the director's assistant, is responsible for much of the management of
location work. One of them, or the unit manager if there is one,
prepares a work of reference that includes maps, addresses,
'phone numbers, train times, schedules of each day's shooting, together with details of where costumes, props and people
need to be each day – even where cars should or should not be
parked. Nothing, except the weather, is left to chance. Time is
money.

Film

A television film crew is smaller than the one that works on a
feature film and is more mobile. Even so it will consist of the
director, his assistant (who is responsible for logging each
shot), the production assistant or floor manager, the cameraman (or lighting-cameraman, as he is usually known) and an
assistant, a sound recordist and an assistant, and all those
required by the design departments. A number of people may
be on hand to deal with additional lighting-requirements,
props and special effects. And, of course, there are the actors.

The procedure is, theoretically, remarkably simple. As the
scene is filmed shot by shot, the design department begins by
preparing the first setting. Lighting is set up. The camera is
put in place. Actors are dressed and made-up. The scene is
rehearsed. Everyone waits for the sun to come out again. The
scene is filmed. That is the theory. In practice, it takes longer.
Scenes must be relit. Scenes must be taken again for the sake
of the cameraman, the sound recordist or even for the actor.
Each 'take' is numbered (e.g. Shot 3, Take 11) and that

number is shown on the clapperboard that is filmed at the beginning of each take and is noted for reference during editing. By the end of the day, a vast number of shots and a few minutes of usable film will be in the can, ready for processing.

Video

A full-size outside-broadcast (OB) unit is not unlike a highly technical travelling circus. The main vehicle is the scanner. This is the size of a furniture-removal van and is air-conditioned. Part of it is 'production control', a small-scale version of a studio control gallery, in which will sit the director and those who assist him, just as they would in a studio gallery (see Chapter 9). Most scanners also contain a tiny soundproof studio, though this is unlikely to be used during the recording of a drama. Another large van will transport the cameras and video-recording equipment. There will be a generator vehicle if there is no electrical power on site, and a number of other back-up vehicles. The technical vehicles are driven by rigger drivers, who are also responsible for the setting-up of the equipment. Also in the cavalcade are mini-buses, cars and caravans, vans bringing props and costumes, lighting and sound equipment. . . .

No two outside broadcasts are exactly the same. One may be to record a garden-party scene for a classical serial. Once the set and equipment have been installed, recording might proceed, much as it would in a studio production. Alternatively the outside broadcast may be indoors, even in a theatre – as it was during the recording of the Royal Shakespeare Company's *The Wars of the Roses* (see also p. 11):

What was needed at Stratford was to give the cameras exactly the kind of freedom and mobility they would enjoy in the studio. To achieve this about half the seats in the stalls were moved, the apron was enlarged so that it pushed right out into the auditorium as a 'thrust' stage, and a vast wooden platform was erected across the stalls area for the cameras and sound booms to manoeuvre on. Even this led to problems of its own, since the cameras had difficulty in pushing their way up the steep rake of the stage and the platform had to be strongly reinforced, since it cracked under the weight of the cameras.

The placing of the cameras could now be dictated by the character of the plays themselves – action in which men scaled walls or delivered long soliloquies while dying on the field of battle. A tower was built at the back of the stage so that a camera could overlook the top of one of the periactoids to give a view over the walls on to the men beneath. Another camera was installed in a pit at the front of the stage to give a kind of death's-eye view. All the other cameras were free to move across the platform and right on to the stage. In addition a hand-held camera was employed so that we could penetrate right into the battle scenes.[1]

When one considers the amount of work involved in turning a theatre into a studio, one must ask such questions as 'Is it worth it?', 'What is gained?', 'Wouldn't it have been easier in a studio?'

There are no general answers. However, almost always one gain is space. There are other benefits. Michael Simpson directed a play by Willy Russell for BBC School Television. It was set in a comprehensive school and its main characters were three teenage boys (played by teenagers new to television). Simpson decided to record it as an OB on location:

Rehearsal began four days before recording and the early decision to record the play on location now produced another bonus. Because it was holiday time and the school was empty, the chance was there for us to rehearse all day, every day, in the actual building. Instead of the usual BBC rehearsal room with sets marked out on the floor in coloured tape, we were able to work from the very beginning in the atmosphere of a deserted school. We could explore, choosing the classroom that would best serve the action of the play, rehearse in those classrooms, use or adapt the furniture that we found, listen to the sounds of our voices, and gently over four days ease Willy's play off the printed page and work it into the school so that school and play grew into one.[2]

Another variation of location work can be seen in the Channel 4 soap opera *Brookside*. Because this was planned as a long-running serial, the production company, Brookside Productions Ltd, decided to buy all thirteen houses in one close or cul-de-sac on a large Merseyside housing-estate. Three of the thirteen houses are terraced 'town houses'. These have been converted so that the upstairs storey of the three contains all the technical equipment needed for the production of the serial. Downstairs are the wardrobe and make-up departments. Another house has been converted into a canteen and one contains post-production facilities. The intervening houses are the 'homes' of the families featured in the serial and all scenes are recorded 'on location' in these houses, and in the close and gardens. A Volvo estate car is used as a mobile unit for recording scenes on other locations. Thus an entire series is recorded and produced on site.

Recent years have seen the continuing miniaturisation of video equipment and, as was described in Chapter 1, many directors have taken to using lightweight units either for short scenes or even for entire productions. One or two lightweight cameras can be used rather in the manner of film cameras, recording a scene shot by shot. They can work either on mains power, trailing on cables from a suitable power source or control van or wander free using battery power. Often the 'headquarters' of such a unit is a Range Rover: large enough, but considerably smaller than the usual scanner.

An even smaller unit was designed for use in the BBC's soap opera *Triangle*, which was set almost entirely on a North Sea ferry. It was not a series that won a lot of praise but technically it was highly innovative:

All the functions of the normal control room were miniaturised and squeezed into a BBC-designed trolley, best described by one of the unit managers Ian Brindle as 'the equivalent of two four-drawer filing cabinets side by side on wheels.' Into this rack was crammed the camera control units, vector and wave-form monitors, colour preview monitors, two tiny monochrome monitors, compact vision and audio mixing panels and space for the VTR.

This trolley could be wheeled around the ship and in the

lift, so the control room could be moved near a particular location. Vision mixer, vision engineer, and sound supervisor sat at the controls with headphones; director, assistant and others perched behind. The entire mini-scanner could operate from one plug on the ship's electricity system, and all the components on the racks were already pre-wired to one another.

With these facilities, the production team managed to record all the scenes for four episodes during a ten-day round-trip, or one episode every two and a half days, which seems highly efficient.[3]

It is too easy a jibe to say that the weaknesses of *Triangle* resulted from using these production techniques. Melodramatic storylines and some less than natural dialogue were more to blame, but the serial did show that location work need not be prohibitively expensive. This point was also made, perhaps somewhat provocatively, by the director David Foster in the trade paper *Broadcast*:

So why is location drama, film or tape so expensive? Is it something to do with the lust for production values by author, producer and director? Is it the feeling of freedom once the studios are left behind? Freedom to do everything? Possibly, and let us whisper it, it is the wish to show off to our peers with extravagant shooting and six-figure budgets.

What production values work for our audience? 200 Extras? Not a lot – it has to be a Ghandi sized crowd or nothing. Crane shots that drift past chimneys? Our audience can take them or leave them. These shots take an hour or two to set up for perhaps 15 seconds of screen time and often their only use is to make other programme makers ask 'Who directed that?'

Suppose we stick to using location to give our story breadth and reality, 'story value' rather than 'production value'? Suppose we make more use of the dub? 'Fix it on the dub' is a joke that obscured the value of that ceremony. In reality, five minutes' careful dubbing can be worth a Cherry Picker and 300 extras, especially if the effect is worked out before the shooting, and not added out of desperation.[4]

That said, television drama would be infinitely the duller were it once again to become studio-bound.

Lighting

It is not enough simply to make an object, actor or scene visible. It must be bright enough for the camera to see. Simply shining one light at an object may make it clear: it can also deprive it of depth or solidity, so lighting must be used to maintain its three-dimensional qualities. A second purpose of lighting is to highlight appropriate characteristics and to conceal or to hide others. It can also be decorative and suggest or reinforce a mood or atmosphere. Consequently the lighting-cameraman is concerned with both technical quality and artistic quality.

As an absolute basis, he has three choices. He can ask for the scene to be played to suit the available light. He can augment available light to meet his purpose. He can start from scratch, relying entirely on his own array of lamps.

On outdoor locations, available light may seem the sensible choice, especially when working with video cameras which can compensate for brightness changes by varying their lens aperture or by adjusting their colour balance. However, problems arise. Strong sunlight can create unwelcome contrasts and areas of deep shadow. It may be possible to record a scene only in the afternoon in a setting best lit by the morning sun. Cloud can result in dull, boring pictures. The midday summer sun is not at the best angle to light an actor's face. It may be a day of constantly changing lighting-conditions in which no two shots would match without recourse to compensatory lighting.

As a first resort, reflectors can be used to direct sunlight onto actors and onto shadowy areas. These are simply large boards either covered in tin foil (which reflects a hard, bright light) or painted white (which reflects a softer light). More practical are portable lighting-units. Small battery-powered lamps are often sufficient to light close-ups and small scenes, but larger areas will require high-intensity lamps powered by a generator or the mains supply. For some scenes however, especially when working with film, one just has to wait for nature.

On indoor locations, existing lighting is almost invariably too weak or wrongly positioned (usually being too high and lighting only the tops of the actors' heads). The lighting-cameraman must therefore rely entirely on his own resources and, fairly obviously, needs to know long before setting out for the location whether the director will be content with a few intimate settings in nooks and crannies of the ancient castle (easy) or whether he expects the viewer to see every corner of the banqueting-hall (expensive).

Sound

When location work is being shot on film, sound-recording equipment (such as a transportable Nagra tape recorder, recording on quarter-inch tape) is required. There must also be a method of synchronising sound and film:

> The tape recorder and camera can be synchronised with each other by one of a number of systems. Normally a pulse is recorded on the ¼-in tape either on a separate track from the programme sound or in some cases across the sound track in such a way that it can be recovered separately. These pulses act rather like the sprocket holes on the picture film. In other words they locate a particular element of the sound track with a particular picture regardless of any slipping or stretching that may have occured to the tape.
>
> Later, in the dubbing theatre, the separate magnetic sound recorder is driven from the pulses recovered from the ¼-in tape so that it is recorded in synchronism with the original picture film.[5]

Video tape of course records both sound and vision.

Microphone technique is similar for both media. The commonest microphone in use is the rifle or gun mike. It is so called because it is shaped like the barrel of a gun or rifle and picks up sound from a very narrow arc but from some distance away. It can therefore be directed at an actor and, while recording his or her speech, excludes a lot of extraneous noise from other directions. It is usually held by a sound assistant by its pistol-type grip, though it may be mounted on a video camera when being used to record close-up scenes or background effects. One of the main problems of outside location work is wind noise. Even a gentle breeze blowing against the mouth of a microphone can cause hefty 'bumps' and other noises to be recorded on the tape. The microphone is therefore usually enclosed in a windshield made of foam rubber and this shield gives it its distinctive bulky shape. Where the sound assistant needs to keep a reasonable distance from the action (to keep out of wide shots on camera), the microphone must be mounted on a boom. If there is much movement in the scene, the boom must be mounted on a small truck which can be wheeled along, provided the ground is fairly level and not too soft. Occasionally it is necessary to lay railway-type tracks for it.

Another technique is the use of radio microphones. Each actor wears a tiny microphone hidden in his jacket or under her blouse or dress. The actor also wears a baby transmitter (carried in a pocket or in a pouch tied round the waist). Each actor's speech can then be transmitted on a different frequency to a receiver in or near the moblie sound-control area. The sound supervisor can then fade in or out each microphone as required, mixing the various sources onto the tape. Radio microphones allow for great mobility and flexibility but are subject to interference from taxi radios, police transmissions, neon lighting and other sources.

Before leaving a location, the sound recordist normally records a certain amount of general 'atmosphere' sound, for use when editing. This can help to link shots together or act as backing to any 'silent' shots.

Specialist Services

A wide range of ancillary back-up services become involved in location work. Besides the more obvious ones (such as lighting-hirers), there are firms that specialise in providing transport for OB work, in providing animals (with handlers and trainers), stunt men (and women), and firms offering aviation and marine services such as underwater and aerial photography, hot-air balloons, divers, underwater explosions and transport for film, equipment, crews and cast.

There are also specialised location caterers, capable of providing not only coffee and rolls but full-scale meals suitable for stars and even gourmet technicians, neither group usually being happy to settle for a sandwich, even half way up Ben Nevis. Even with such on-site services, a vital component of every OB's equipment remains an Egon Ronay or *Good Food Guide*.

9.

In the Studio

Pleasurable though location work may be, much of television drama is still made in studios, mainly for economic reasons. Studios are not cheap, either. Little ones cost £0.5 million and big ones rather more. Harlech Television's new complex at Cardiff (due to be completed in 1984) is a £15 million investment, with studio and control equipment costing £3.5 million (for two studios). With such capital investment, it is no wonder that broadcasting-organisations want the best use out of their facilities. It is generally agreed that the BBC's eight studios at its London Television Centre are the fastest television-production factory in Europe:

> All eight studios must handle light entertainment, drama, live shows complete with studio audience and children's programmes. With such demand and high turnover of programmes scheduling of studio resources has to be completed at least nine months in advance. This leaves few opportunities for flexibility – except when topical events demand the 'override facility'.
>
> Recent arguments have called for phasing out of the multi-purpose studio because of its expense and inflexibility. But the BBC claim to have overcome these problems by refining the programme production factory approach, investing in saturation lighting rigs and using motorised scenery hoists.[1]

(Saturation lighting means sufficient lamps to meet all likely requirements without re-rigging.)

All the lamps can be controlled electronically from the

studio floor. This means that lighting for one production can be changed to another in about two hours.

Liason engineer, Derek Robinson, says it would take a whole day using the conventional telescope system. 'Adopting a saturation rig will pay off simply because of the time it saves. Now we can aim for half an hour of finished output every 24 hours.'

A 50-minute episode of *By the Sword Divided* [a serial about the Civil War], with its complicated set, would take three days.

Many of those involved in the creative processes of television would say that there was nothing to be proud of in such factory-line methods. The unyielding schedules must, they say, mean indifferent standards and shambolic haste to get final scenes on tape before someone pulls the plugs out and a set is struck. Another view is taken by the director John Glenister, apparently aware of the financial pressures that lie upon managements and of the fact that drama is one of the most expensive forms of television:

The only way we're going to do quality stuff, and to be allowed to continue to do quality television, is to get in on time and on budget. It's no good getting all artistic and saying, 'I need ten weeks to make this ten second scene.'[2]

To get a play on tape on time requires, as we have seen, much forward planning and an army of artists, performers and technicians. What the studio days mean for many of those involved in the making of a play will have become apparent by this point. In this chapter therefore we shall simply attempt to summarise the roles of those involved on a recording-day, assuming a set has been erected, dressed and lit. (For a major drama, one day is set aside for this setting and lighting – no more.)

The Gallery

The gallery or control room is above the studio floor. It may be possible to see part of the studio floor from the gallery, but everyone in the gallery relies on the bank of television monitor screens in front of the control desk. If there are four cameras involved in the production then four of these screens will always show the output of those cameras. Another will show any captions that are being generated electronically, another any slides, and on other screens the director (and others) can preview any film (telecine) or pre-recorded video inserts to be played into the production. The central screen shows which picture (or combination of pictures) is going onto the tape (or being transmitted in a live production).

At the centre of the desk sits the director. Besides seeing all the monitors, he can hear studio sound as it is being recorded. He also has audio links with other production departments and with technicians on the floor, and especially with the floor manager or production assistant. The director is not only preoccupied with seeing that the play is performed as he wishes and recorded as he wishes. It is his task to inspire the entire team and to maintain the enthusiasm necessary to achieve the day's target. Because he is a creative artist and because recording is the climax of a lengthy and absorbing process, he is allowed to have a number of explosive tantrums during the day.

On one side of him sits a nimble-fingered genius. This is the vision mixer, who has a dauntingly complex control panel in front of him or her. It is the vision mixer's job to watch all six or seven monitor screens and cut, fade, wipe or mix from one source to another at exactly the moment that was decided in advance and which is noted in the camera script which the vision mixer is now too busy to read. The vision mixer must also anticipate the director's changes of mind. It helps to have the manual dexterity of a concert pianist, the eyes of a lynx and the memory of a computer.

On the other side of the director is his assistant. She notes all 'takes', changes to the script and timings for use during editing. In a live production, she is responsible for time-keeping and for seeing the production ends on time. Timing is less crucial on a recorded play, which can be edited if it 'spreads' once it is in the studio. She must also remind the director of those things which he has asked to be reminded about and which she thinks it will be diplomatic to mention.

There are other people in the main control room. An electronic-effects operator may be sitting at a computer terminal, generating effects at the required moment. There is a technical supervisor or manager watching for picture quality. A make-up supervisor sees how the cast look on camera and the costume designer watches how the costumes look on camera and notes how the cast are failing to wear them to their best effect. Both are ready to go down to the floor to make final adjustments before recording. The designer is depressed by the director's perversity in pointing cameras at characters and not at the best bits of the set. The silent person unable to sit down who occasionally communicates unhappiness by falling very silent is the producer. The small, neurotic heap in the corner is the writer.

Next door to main control, viewable through a window and in touch by means of an audio-link is sound control. In charge is the sound supervisor. At his control desk, he can 'open' and 'close' each microphone on the studio floor, fading one up, one down, achieving the optimum sound balance. He is responsible for the technical quality of the sound (that it is of a level suitable for broadcasting and devoid of distortion and interference) and the artistic quality (the balancing of different speakers to reflect their perspectives and positions on the screen and the balance of voices with sound effects and music). His control desk gives him the facility of prehearing the level of a sound source before mixing it onto the programme tape.

Also in sound control are sound assistants who play in recorded sound effects and music from tapes or discs. Sound control is also responsible for playing such effects through speakers onto the studio floor when necessary, through what is known as 'foldback'.

In another control room the other side of the main control is lighting control. Here the lighting-engineers operate a console which controls all the studio lights. These must obviously be changed as recording moves from scene to scene and set to set. They may have to be altered during a scene when, for example, someone enters a room and switches on a light or (more gradually) to suggest the onset of evening.

Also in lighting control (or 'racks', as it is traditionally known) are the engineers responsible for adjusting and controlling picture quality from the cameras. The exposure and tonal qualities of each camera must be adjusted constantly to match one camera to another. Exposure can also be increased or decreased to achieve specific effects. So too can the tone of a camera. 'Crushing' the tone (making it blacker) will help to achieve a night effect or deep shadows.

Finally, in a separate area (either adjacent to the gallery or in another part of the building) is the video suite, where recording-engineers supervise the actual recording of the play and the quality of the recording. After each scene has been recorded they make a quick 'spot check' of the tape and, if all is well, give a 'clear' to the director, who then passes the good news on to the studio floor.

The Studio Floor

The various sets arranged around the studio often have a curiously disconnected air about them and a visitor might be forgiven for wondering how they could possibly all belong to the same play. Some larger sets do however look marvellous 'in real life' as well as on the screen, and many a designer's efforts have been rewarded by intrigued murmurs of admiration from technicians and actors when they first see the realisation of the origianl plans and models. Even if there has been a full day for setting and lighting, and even though recording is due to start soon, carpenters and set dressers will still be hammering away or repositioning drapes – sometimes right through final rehearsals, to be stopped only when recording begins.

Just as obvious as the sets to the visitor are the cameras: four or five of them for a major drama production. In spite of their size, they can glide fluently around the studio. When one is moved to follow an actor, it is said to be tracking. Sideways movement is known as crabbing. In any given position, a camera can be moved in various ways on its pedestal. Its height can be raised or lowered, it can look up or down (tilting) and it can turn from side to side (panning). Its lens can be moved in and out (zooming) to give close-ups and long shots. Occasionally a camera is mounted on what is basically a small crane to give it greater movement and elevation. On top of each camera is a tiny monitor screen in which the cameraman can see the shot he is offering to the director (and vision mixer). All camera movements must be carefully rehearsed in advance and special attention is paid to any movements (for example, tracking, panning, zooming) which happen while that camera's shot is being recorded. A red light on top of each camera shines when that camera's shot is being taken.

Also on the studio floor, there is usually at least one boom microphone. This microphone is suspended from a long extendible pole, itself mounted on a moblie platform (sometimes called the boom pram) and it can be moved in a variety of ways to catch the dialogue of the actors and (we hope) to keep out of the camera's view and to avoid casting a shadow on any actor or scenery.

The visitor to a television studio is almost always amazed by the array of lighting. The entire ceiling seems to be a close-packed array of lamps. This lighting-grid hangs just below the ceiling and lamps are clamped, clipped or slung from the lattice structure of tubular steel. Access is possible via cat-walks. Larger studios (such as those used for drama) often have a series of independently suspended bars (known as barrels) which can be raised and lowered. Besides actual spotlights, there are a number of 'soft lights', perhaps attached to expanding pantographs. There are many lamps on remotely controlled expanding poles which can also be lowered from the grid. Many of the lamps have 'barn doors' fitted around their lens. These four shutters can be adjusted to control the amount and the direction of the light. A number of lamps on telescopic floor stands, mounted on castors, may be in use to give upward lighting, to light particular areas of scenery or perhaps to provide the imitation sunlight that must shine through windows or doors when they are opened. There may also be rows of lamps on the ground ('ground rows') hidden behind scenery to provide particular effects. Again in the minutes up to final rehearsals (and between rehearsals and takes) electricians and lighting-men adjust individual lamps. Some alterations are rapid, minor adjustments which can be achieved in a break between rehearsals. Others are lengthier processes, when everyone has to stand around while one person uses a telescopic pole to adjust a sequence of lamps which (despite all the planning) fail to give the desired effect on scenery and actors. Now that more and more lighting-grids contain power-controlled lamps, and with the installation of saturation rigs (see p. 128), such adjustments are usually just a matter of 'fine tuning' and it is rarely necessary actually to move lamps.

As we have said, the person in charge of all operations on the studio floor is the production assistant (BBC) or floor manager (ITV). He (or she) is the director's representative and wears a two-way headset which allows him to hear what is being said in the gallery and (provided he depresses a switch) to speak to the director. This is a radio device: he is not anchored by a cable. Obviously the floor manager cannot speak to the gallery while recording is in process unless he tiptoes away from the action and whispers out of the range of the studio microphones. With a script constantly in his hands, he must ensure everything runs smoothly, calmly and on time. A good floor manager is strict, good-humoured and tactful. It is his job to relay instructions to the prop men, to ensure there is silence at the right moment and to translate the director's instructions to the cast. For example, when the director yells, 'For the tenth bloody time, tell that little creep not to sit on the edge of the sofa like some constipated chimpanzee', the floor manager politely suggests the actor lean back in the sofa 'just for the cameras'. There is an assistant floor manager whose main job is to see that the members of the cast are where they should be at the right moment.

Besides the cameramen (and their assistants, who may be required to move cables at particular moments), electricians, set dressers, prop men, make-up assistants and others already mentioned, there are the sound floor assistants. One is responsible for the fitting of any radio microphones that individual actors may be wearing and for the positioning of microphones hidden in such items of scenery as the bowl of flowers or a lampshade. Others operate the boom and its 'pram', and their movements will have been planned carefully in advance:

The positioning of the cameras and booms is decided at a planning meeting prior to the production day attended by the director, sound supervisor, lighting director, set designer and any other specialists concerned at that stage in the proceedings. It is explained that the marked position can give only an approximate indication of the starting position because both cameras and booms are mobile. No matter how careful the planning, shots develop and positions become modified as the result of rehearsal experience. Nevertheless it is necessary to have a pretty firm basis from which to work. During the course of a production the cameras and booms will probably be required to work in a variety of different areas and these are identified on the plan by the camera numbers or boom letters and position numbers (i.e. cam. 1 pos. A; boom A pos. 2, etc.).[3]

Besides microphones, the sound department is responsible for spot effects (i.e. sound effects created on the spot in the studio). These might involve the slamming of an effects door off camera (because the one on the set does not make the right noise) or the ringing of a bell or buzzer. Telephones that must ring on cue and be answered in vision are usually properly wired up and operated by a device known as a telephone ringer which ensures that the 'phone will ring instantly it is required. 'Sound' is also in charge of all the talkback system: director's talkback to floor manager and cameramen, lighting talkback from racks to lighting-electricians on the floor, sound talkback from gallery to sound floor assistants, and all the reverse talkback from the floor to the different sections in the gallery.

Eventually everything is ready. The scene has been rehearsed for the last time. Make-up rushes in and dabs at an actor. A shout from the floor manager. 'Quiet please on the floor.' The red light goes on over the studio door. Back in the gallery the order is given to the video recordists, 'Start the tape.' The director's assistant speaks to the floor manager. 'Ten, nine, eight, seven . . . Cue!'

With editing now as easy and as sophisticated as it is, there is little to be gained from frenetic attempts to record long chunks of the play. Artistically that might be very satisfying but technically it is just not worth it. Consequently, once in the studio, almost every play is broken up into sequences which are reheased and then recorded one by one. These sequences may be very short, they may be complete scenes, or even two or three scenes played as one sequence.

, Even with the best planning and with the greatest industry and cooperation imaginable, it is sometimes just not possible to record all these sequences on time. A camera breaks down, there is a union meeting, a special effect will not work. . . . The director wonders if there is any chance of an over-run, which may mean working through till ten o'clock, with a hundred people on overtime. If an overrun is absolutely vital, and is granted, will the director ever be employed again? Ultimately the director knows that management would rather have an expensive completed play than waste the fifty minutes already recorded. He knows too that this will not be allowed to become a habit and so, amazingly, the production is quite often completed on time. It is still only a jigsaw of separated scenes, voice-overs, retakes, fluffs and alternative shots; but it is all there, on tape or film. There is time to sort it out later: now it is time for everyone to unwind.

'Marvellous! You were absolutely right.'

'Thanks for a lovely script.'

'It was the costumes that made it.'

'Nonsense – the sets were out of this world.'

'That scene on the sofa. Perfect.'

'Another drink?'

10.
Post-production

'Post-production' simply refers to those stages through which the various pieces of film and tape must pass before they become a completed play ready for transmission.

Film-editing

Compared with many processes in television, film-editing is an ancient craft, having arrived in television from the cinema. In both industries it is fundamentally the same process.

Put in its simplest terms, it consists of a film editor using the sight and sound of the clapperboard closing to synchronise pictures with sound. Once that moment is 'in sync', then so will be the rest of the shot. He then uses a simple cutting and joining device, known as a joiner, to cut the film up into strips. These are identified and (using the log recorded during filming) the selected takes are assembled in the required order. To join two pieces of film, the editor places them in the joiner, where they are held by sprockets which match the holes in the film. Sticky tape is placed over the edges of the film, the joiner is punched down and the two pieces of film are one. Unwanted film is put on one side and kept, 'just in case we need it'.

The first assemblage of shots, the 'rough cuts', gives some idea of the final sequence. Now the director and editor work together on 'fine editing'. They must decide how quickly one shot must follow the previous one, when to linger on a departing figure, when to cut quickly to the next scene. Too many rapid jump cuts can confuse the viewer, but if the action is slow then the viewer may dismiss the film with that dreaded insult, 'It's boring!' In practice, much of the excitement of a film is created at this stage, simply by the way it is cut. For many film makers, these are the joyful hours: deciding when to slip in a reaction shot or telling close-up, when to hold a plaintive scene or create chilling irony through a striking juxtaposition of images, when to freeze a frame, when to use slow motion or a gentle dissolve. . . . If only time permitted, this agonising and debating could go on for ever. However a final cut is decided upon and sent off to the laboratories. When the prints have been returned, the final dubbing-sessions can begin.

These involve the adding of music (which may have been especially commissioned: some notable scores have been composed for television drama, such as Geoffrey Burgon's themes for the BBC's *Tinker, Tailor, Soldier, Spy* and for Granada Television's production of *Brideshead Revisited*) and also sound effects, where required. All the various soundtracks, including the dialogue, are mixed together by the dubbing-mixer under the supervision of the director. Following this, the laboratories produce the show print which is the film ready for transmission – or at least for conversion in a telecine suite from film to video for actual transmission on a television network. (This final conversion does not substantially alter its nature: it remains a 'film' because of the way in which it has been made.)

A modified version of the above process is applied to film sequences which are to be edited into a studio play.

Video-editing

In the early days of video-taping, it was possible to edit tape only by cutting it. There were problems. Not the smallest was the fact that the impulses of the sound and pictures were about half a second apart on the tape. Any edit point was therefore some sort of compromise between the dictates of sound and vision for the best cutting-point. Few can have looked forward to tape-editing, but at least it was possible to cut together chunks of a play into one coherent whole. Obviously you could not easily add 'cut-aways' (i.e. reaction shots) and the whole process was distinctly unsubtle. No wonder film became the preferred medium.

Nowadays video tape is edited electronically. To do this, at least two video recorders are needed. One plays the tape that is to be edited. The second re-records those elements of the recording that are to be preserved. It is therefore simple to erase a 'fluff' or mistake and to move up the retake to run on from a point just before the fluff. In Figure 2, let us suppose the section A–B is to be edited out. The second recorder records from the first recorder up to point A and is then stopped. The first tape runs on to point B and the second recorder starts up again at that point.

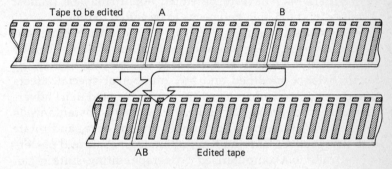

FIGURE 2   Video-tape editing

The process is not as cumbersome as might be first thought. Indeed it can be a very speedy process, held up only by the director needing time to think. It is also very precise. 'Close it up just a gnat's' (meaning let's make B happen a micro-second sooner after A) is a phrase regularly heard in editing-suites, and one that is easily acted on.

Much of this speed is due to the use of time-coding. This system identifies all recordings by real time (as expressed by the twenty-four hour clock). During recording, the director's assistant (either on location or in the gallery) is constantly noting the times of possible or necessary editing-points on her script. The matching time code is visible on the editing-copy of the tape when it is in the editing-suite. Consequently a line of dialogue that was fluffed at 1647' 20" and re-recorded at 1650' 35" (i.e. hours, minutes and seconds) can be quickly located in the reels of tape that contain the play.

The play's production assistant may prepare a roughly edited version of the play. Alternatively this may be done by the editor working from production notes. The director has a cassette copy of the roughly edited play, so he can decide what needs to be done to bring it up to the best standard possible when the time comes for fine editing. Just as with a film, it may lack pace; a particular scene which everyone loved in rehearsal may now seem simply an indulgence. A performance may not have come up to scratch and some of that actor's part may have to be edited out. It may be (almost certainly it is) too long and needs to be edited to time.

Sophisticated editing-suites can do more than erase unwanted moments. For example, a detail of a picture can be expanded to full screen size, the tone of a picture altered, the colour balance modified and any number of special effects added. As one commercial editing-suite boasted in its advertisements, the director can take advantage of 'Instantaneous squeeze, zoom, freeze, flip, tumble, invert, ooze, and rotate with perspective; Chroma Key, ultimate, mosaic and posterisation', and in a computerised video-tape editing-suite he can use 'multiple vision mixer effects with up to eight VTRs controlled for complex effects to minimise multi generation, 16mm/35mm telecines, electronic paintbox and animation disc and electronic titling'.

The trouble is, that sort of video-editing suite is expensive to equip and therefore to use. The cost of two hours' editing-time in one of the many similar commercial post-production facilities that have opened up in and around London may be the same as a week spent in a film-editing suite.

A director must consequently spend a lot of time with a cassette player, imagining and planning what he will do to his rough-edited tapes in the editing-suite, so that time there is used as economically as possible. However, most directors want to try out things before making final decisions. As it is too expensive to experiment in what is called an on-line editing-suite, it seems likely that there will be an increase in off-line editing-suites. On-line suites offer the full range of editing-facilities; off-line suites offer a much more limited range. In *Broadcast* magazine in mid 1983, Robin Shenfield reported on the situation then:

> The high cost of on-line looks like being a problem that is here to stay. However economic it might be to shoot on video, in the editing room the equation goes right out of the window. On their own admission some facilities are far too expensive.
>
> Directors are keener than ever to juggle film and video in novel off-line combinations to give them the time they need but cannot afford to buy in off-line. And it's not a problem unique to the independent facilities. The BBC has only two off-line suites at TV Centre – and it likes to keep one of those in reserve. The current three to four hour editing ceiling on a 90-minute drama is enough to deter many that might go to video sooner. . . .
>
> Even pioneering broadcasters like LWT which made a spurt of video dramas a few years ago, are drawing back into film because of the high costs of video editing.[1]

In that same edition of *Broadcast*, a number of directors and editors speculated on post-production trends as they appeared at that time. For example, Geoff Posner, a BBC director working in the field of light entertainment, welcomed the prospect of more off-line facilities:

> I think off-line editing is one area that has to grow in future. Equipment is coming onto the market now that could be operated by production staff, and that makes the economics very attractive. I've directed a couple of shows at the BBC recently where it would have been nice to off-line first. The problem is that there is not always the time or the resources.[2]

The costs of video-editing also impinge on the world of commercials. A specialist commercial director, Jim Baker, praised the efficiency of film-editing:

We regularly cost productions on film and video and on this
strictly comparable basis film emerges as the most controllable and also the most economic route. . . . Every time you
go into a video editing suite you get clobbered by the heavy
machinery rate. If editing facilities want to move in the right
direction they should scrap all this £300-an-hour business
and work on a day rate.

We get into a lot of complex productions with fast film
cutting that is impossible to do on video. You can use a video
house for fast assembly and do all your opticals, your
dissolves and wipes, but effects and fast cuts are better done
on film.[3]

At the time of writing, it seems likely that there may be a
marriage of convenience between the two media. A situation-
comedy series was one early experiment in blending film- and
video-editing techniques, an experiment described by its producer, Brian Eastman:

We decided to edit *Father's Day*, the series we made for
Channel 4, on film even though it was shot on video. It was
the method that best suited our style of shooting.

With a single video camera we shot the whole series
multi-episodically, in much the same way you would shoot
a film. After each take the director, Leszek Burzynski,
nominated which shot he wanted printed.

From the master tapes, the film lab transferred only the
selected takes onto black-and-white film. From there we
went into the film cutting room. We did it that way because
it's easier to assemble this kind of programme from a
straight line of film than do it off-line and then on-line in
video. Video-tape editing is more appropriate when material is in some kind of order, when it has been vision mixed to
some extent. We needed the linear approach of a film editor
for what was very much a film-style production.

We did a complete edit on film and then took it along to
TVi [a facilities company] for final assembly on video,
adding the few bits of digital effects that were needed. TVi
said there was no way they would have cut the show in the

same way. We were rather pleased by that because we were after a fresh and original treatment.

By editing film rather than video, we got about four times as much editing as we would have in a video off-line suite. We needed that extra time to play around with the cuts, especially because it was a show in which we were trying new things.[4]

It seems likely that, where light entertainment and commercial directors have led, drama directors and producers must follow. Some directors have appreciated just what can be done with video-editing and are prepared to work fast enough to achieve what they want in the time available. It remains a fact that some are more conservative:

Those film-trained directors that already have reservations about video as a production tool, find them compounded in editing. Video-editing – how many times has it been said – is not under the same level of control nor has the same feel.[5]

What we must now appreciate perhaps is that those who fully understand video-editing, the video-tape editors themselves, be admitted as one more member of the creative team that makes a play. To quote two experienced editors,

Ten years ago the editor was lucky to get a credit. He was just the person who bolted it all together. But, as the capabilities of post-production improved, he's become far more central.[6]

The editor's job is to be the link between the director and the programme. Every job that comes in is very different. Some directors want to use you as a neg cutter, others want as much creative input as you can give them. I enjoy both. I don't understand directors who say they can do 90% of what's required with their hands behind their back. They must be very bored. . . . When videotape editing started out it was just a kind of invisible mending job. It's come on a long way since then.[7]

When director and editor have completed the final edit, when the dubbing of the various extra sound tracks (such as the music) has been finished, then the video play (like the film) is ready for transmission. All it needs now is an audience.

11.
The Audience

So, with a mixture of inspiration, hard graft, traumas and tender loving care, the television drama is made. In some way or other, perhaps two hundred or more people have made a contribution to its genesis and production. It now exists, whether it is a beautifully crafted film (every frame a Rembrandt), a single play (society will never be the same again), an episode of a series (plot the same as last week, different villains), a sumptuous classic serial (costumes on exhibition at Stately Towers, Sundays and Bank Holidays only) or an episode of a soap (will Daphne decide to keep the stray cat or will everyone simply offer advice?). A publicity machine is put into operation to ensure the largest possible audience. The play is trailed regularly on the network on which it is to be shown. Details are published in programme journals such as *Radio Times* and *TV Times*. Journalists are sometimes invited to see the production in advance of transmission, so that they may preview it in their paper, it is hoped favourably (more of which later). Press officers of the production house in question compile lengthy press releases (an excited blurb, a calmer plot synopsis, biographies of the cast, a whimsical paragraph about the author and how he/she got the idea for the play when he/she underwent a similar experience – 'No, I can honestly say it's not autobiographical'), and distribute these wads of duplicated prose to every paper that has a television column. And then the play is transmitted.

In 5 million homes around the country, a television set is switched on. In 40 per cent of those homes, the set is switched to that channel. In one of those homes the supposedly 'average couple' decides to watch. After a minute, she remembers she left the stove on and pops back into the kitchen for a minute. A line in the play reminds him about something that happened at work. They talk. They watch again. The 'phone rings. He turns the sound down a bit and she answers. Just a short conversation. Turn the sound up . . . . And the next day, if they are asked if they watched the play, what do they say? 'Of course we did. Yes, we had it on. Yes, yes, we saw it. It was just before that other thing – or was it after the news? It was about . . . What was it about?'

In contrast there are those viewers (perhaps a smaller percentage than programme makers like to think) for whom watching a television play or episode of a series or serial is an event, planned for in advance, viewed attentively and even considered afterwards. With the spread of domestic video recorders, there is the likelihood that this type of viewer will become more common as people learn to shunt plays to times more convenient to themselves than to the programme planners. It remains a fact however that for a very large proportion of the viewing public, television drama is part of the unending stream of entertainment and information that pours out of the box in the corner. It is no more special than a favoured quiz show, *Match of the Day* or *Panorama*. And yet. . . .

Television drama (especially series and serials) is popular. Whether the viewers give it their undivided attention or not, it is a strange week in which half the 'top twenty' peak-time programmes are not some sort of made-for-television dramas. So can anything useful be said about the audience, about how it regards and what it expects of television drama, and about the makers of television drama and their relationship to their audience? Or is it too vast a topic to cover in a book that is no more than an introduction to the subject?

Some things can and indeed must be said. First, it must be stressed that television drama does not exist in a vacuum: as the signal leaves the transmitter, it is not lost in space and time. It is viewed. What is more, it is viewed in the home. This apparent platitude can be easily forgotten by those whose business is television, whether they are involved in it as programme makers or as students of (and commentators on) the medium. For them, viewing is often a corporate act. The play is watched critically, perhaps in a preview theatre, perhaps in a lecture room, quite likely on a cassette and in the middle of the day. It is their business to talk about it, perhaps to joke about it; certainly to make sense of it and to put it in some sort of critical perspective.

Many people (adults as well as children) have no chance to do this. Many (often the young, frequently the elderly) watch alone. Even in homes where family viewing is the norm, the play is often followed by 'the next thing', be it the next programme or the washing-up, while its images can fester in the subconscious. Rational discussion, appreciation and assessment are rare. Now I am aware that this argument may strike some readers as being offensively paternalistic or patronising, but I believe it is easy to underestimate the impact of drama and perhaps especially the impact of well-made drama, be it a soap opera, a glossy thriller or a prestigious play. As John Ellis, a teacher of film studies at the University of Kent, has noted in his analysis of the cinema and broadcast television,

> TV drama presents a gallery of characters in their own domestic settings, or quasi-domestic settings, all of whom are in some way abnormal (hence their comic or dramatic interest). Their abnormality confirms the normality of both the viewer and the viewer's presumed setting. The TV viewer is thus a viewer who is confirmed as isolated, even insulated, from the events of an outside world which is defined in opposition to the domestic and familial setting in which TV viewing is assumed to take place. Broadcast TV is thus in a position to be disturbing for its viewers when it represents something that is repressed in most domestic situations.[1]

One implication of that point has been well articulated by the former head of the BBC Television Drama Group, Shaun Sutton:

> Television invades man's privacy to an extent he would not tolerate from friend or neighbour. Drama, traditionally the host of the evening's entertainment, is now the guest in the house. As such, it should assume the graces and responsibilities of a guest.[2]

But what if it should discard those graces and responsibilities?

'If a play offends it is an assault within the home and its outrage is the greater';[3] and, as John Ellis succinctly noted:

> The largest scandals about TV broadcasts have occurred in Britain when a few TV programmes have dared to represent activities which are censured or go unrepresented in many families. Thus scandals erupted about representations of sexuality, violence and the use of censored words, swear-words. In producing representations of such often-repressed elements, TV came closest to upsetting the confirmation of the viewer's position.[4]

It is tempting to dismiss those who feel that family life as we know it is destroyed by a bare bum on 'Play for Today' and to sympathise with the writer of a letter published in the *Guardian* newspaper some years ago:

> Sir, —I think there should be more sex on television. I pay my £6 like anyone else and I don't see why I shouldn't get what I want. At present the BBC is too concerned with producing cultural programmes of middle-brow rubbish, like the Val Doonican Show.
>
> It's high time we got something we can get our teeth into, like a good strip show. I suggest we have it after 'Match of the Day' on Saturday night.
>
> Yours faithfully, etc.

Yet it remains a fact that many people are offended, genuinely and deeply, by a swear word, a blasphemy or the unexpected sight of part of the human anatomy not often seen – and certainly not in the lounge. Faced with that attitude, many programme makers might be tempted to go out of their way to shock deliberately. Indeed it is possible to think of some programmes, some plays, which have been little more than exhibitionistic. It is sad that such (isolated) examples of bad taste have played into the hands of those who wish to limit the freedoms of programme makers, freedoms recognised by, (for example) the Independent Broadcasting Authority in the *Guidelines* it lays down for programme makers on the use of bad language, 'sex' and nudity:

Language

Writers, producers and performers seek, with reason, to protect their freedom of expression. It is therefore important, if this freedom is not to be jeopardised, to avoid the gratuitous use of language likely to offend.

There is no absolute ban on the use of bad language. But when used it must be defensible in terms of context and authenticity. Many people who would not be unduly shocked by swearing are offended when it is used to excess and without justification.

Sex and nudity

The same considerations apply here as to bad language. Popular entertainment and comedy have always relied to some extent on sexual innuendo and ambiguous (or suggestive) gesture and behaviour: but this does not justify mere crudity. Much of the world's great drama and fiction has been concerned with love and passion, and it would be wrong (if not impossible) to require writers to renounce all intention to shock or disturb: but the aim should be to move, not to offend. The portrayal of sexual behaviour, and of nudity, needs to be defensible in context and presented with tact and discretion.[5]

Such a code is not a sell-out to the prudes who would wish to control or censor everything that appears on the screen. It is a defence against those individuals and groups whose attacks on drama (and other programmes) are emotional and illogical; against those who feel that physical love under the regulation duvet is offensive but who do not object to murder in close-up; against those who do not object to the pirate getting paralytic on grog and carving up half his crew with a cutlass but are outraged by a seventeen-year-old enjoying half a pint of lager and walking home quietly.

Throughout this book we have been discussing broadcast television, i.e. transmitted programmes available to the public (which may be extended to include freely-available channels disseminated by cable or satellite). As we turn to the question of violence on the television screen, it is difficult to exclude video tapes, which became widely available in the early eighties and which at first were subject to very little control.

Now it is easy to say that parents should ensure that children are protected from 'unsuitable' programmes (be they transmitted or on tape), that those who know they are prone to nightmares should not watch a play or film that is fairly obviously going to be gruesome, and that (just as the *Guardian* reader implies he would not mind a giggle at a strip show late at night) so an 'adult' viewer should be allowed 'a bit of violence on the box'.

It is not so simple. Parents do, either thoughtlessly or by neglect, allow young children to see programmes not intended for them. We are not all as emotionally mature as we might like to think, violent crimes may 'give people ideas' and witnessing the repetition of brutish acts can blunt a person's sensitivity. Whatever we may like to think, there is cause for concern on these grounds, as the IBA *Guidelines* point out:

(a) At the simplest level, some portrayed acts of violence may go beyond the bounds of what is tolerable for the average viewer. These could be classified as material which, in the words of the Act, 'offends against good taste or decency' or 'is likely to be offensive to public feeling'.

(b) There is portrayed violence which is potentially so disturbing that it might be psychologically harmful, particularly for young or emotionally insecure viewers.

(c) Violence portrayed on television may be imitated in real life.

(d) The regular and recurrent spectacle of violence might lead viewers to think violence in one form or another has been given the stamp of approval. Once violence is thus accepted and tolerated people will, it is believed, tend to become more callous, more indifferent to the suffering imposed on the victims of violence.[6]

Fairly obviously it makes good sense not to include scenes in a play for young viewers which children might see and copy. While children do not in fact have access to cutlasses, they can obtain broken bottles, bricks, knives and ropes. It is not good sense to show scenes which make clear how these can be used to inflict pain or death. But what of the scene in a detective series which showed how a criminal shot his enemy from a particular motorway bridge, a scene copied in real life a few days later? Can the writer, director and producer dismiss the coincidence with a clear conscience? But would not television drama be unbearably boring if any potentially dangerous violent action was edited out? What producer could take account of a real-life lunatic on a motorway bridge?

To ban all guns from television because of that one ghastly occurrence is irrational. To say that what is shown on television after eleven o'clock at night must be edited with eight-year-olds in mind is nannyish in the extreme, yet the effect of every act of violence shown on the screen must be evaluated before transmission. More importantly perhaps, the overall frequency of violent acts in television fiction must be subject to scrutiny.

Statistics can be compiled to prove almost any point, but, as George W. Brandt admits in his introduction to *British Television Drama*, 'Some research (not unchallenged, it's only fair to say) has come to the conclusion that disturbing incidents on the TV screen *may* rub off on behaviour in certain age groups.'[7] He goes on to quote H. J. Eysenck and D. K. B. Nias, who state:

The evidence strongly indicates that the portrayal of sex and violence in the media does affect the attitude and behaviour of viewers; that these effects are variable, depending on the details of presentation and the personality of the viewers; and that recommendations for action depend on the person's value system.[8]

So why show violent action in drama? The IBA *Guidelines* give a clear answer:

First, conflict is of the essence of drama, and conflict often leads to violence. Second, the real world contains much violence in many forms, and when television seeks to reflect the world – in fact or in fiction – it would be unrealistic and untrue to ignore its violent aspects.[9]

That admitted, the IBA provides a code for its programme makers which, like its guidelines on language and sex, is a protection for both the viewer and the producer:

The Content of the Programme Schedule as a Whole
(a) People seldom view just one programme. An acceptable minimum of violence in each individual programme may add up to an intolerable level over a period.
(b) The time of screening of each programme is important. Adults may be expected to tolerate more than children can. The ITV policy of 'family viewing time' until 9 pm entails special concern for younger viewers.

The Ends and the Means
(c) There is no evidence that the portrayal of violence for good or 'legitimate' ends is likely to be less harmful to the individual, or to society, than the portrayal of violence for evil ends.

Presentation
(d) There is no evidence that 'sanitised' or 'conventional' violence, in which the consequences are concealed, minimized or presented in a ritualistic way, is innocuous. It may be just as dangerous to society to conceal the results of violence or to minimize them as to let people see clearly the full consequences of violent behaviour, however gruesome: what may be better for society may be emotionally more upsetting or more offensive for the individual viewer.
(e) Violence which is shown as happening long ago or far away may seem to have less impact on the viewer, but it remains violence. Horror in costume remains horror.
(f) Dramatic truth may occasionally demand the portrayal of a sadistic character, but there can be no defence of violence shown solely for its own sake, or of the gratuitous exploitation of sadistic or other perverted practices.
(g) Ingenious and unfamiliar methods of inflicting pain or injury – particularly if capable of easy imitation – should not be shown without the most careful consideration.

(h) Violence has always been and still is widespread throughout the world, so violent scenes in news and current affairs programmes are inevitable. But the editor or producer must be sure that the degree of violence shown is essential to the integrity and completeness of his programme.

The Young and the Vulnerable
(i) Scenes which may unsettle young children need special care. Insecurity is less tolerable for a child – particularly an emotionally unstable child – than for a mature adult. Violence, menace and threats can take many forms – emotional, physical and verbal. Scenes of domestic friction, whether or not accompanied by physical violence, can easily cause fear and insecurity.
(j) Research evidence shows that the socially or emotionally insecure individual, particularly if adolescent, is specially vulnerable. There is also evidence that such people tend to be more dependent on television than are others. Imagination, creativity or realism on television cannot be constrained to such an extent that the legitimate service of the majority is always subordinated to the limitations of a minority. But a civilized society pays special attention to its weaker members.[10]

The Code concludes with a warning that programme makers are responsible for their own decisions. Sometimes they will decide to go against the Code (or its BBC equivalent). Shaun Sutton would appear not to encourage such a decision, even if it were to be taken consciously in order to make a dramatic point:

Going over the violent top may be the result of inexperience rather than a sinister sadism in the director. He may have convinced himself that, in order to push home the moral of his drama, he must show the pain to be overwhelming. Experience would have told him that precisely the same effect could have been gained subtly; and if experience didn't, his producer should have.[11]

He clearly believes in the responsibility of the producer: 'That

drama is fiction in no way releases its producers from responsibility. One cannot hide behind that convenient old shield,
"It's only a play. . .".'[12] But then, one might add, as a producer
he would, wouldn't he?

The playwright David Hare is caustic about such attitudes
and about the BBC, which he believes is 'run almost exclusively by ex-journalists':

> They appear actually to believe in something they call
> responsibility, which by the time it reaches our screens we
> may take to mean blandness, and in something else called
> editorial control, which I construe as them knowing better
> than you do, something which an artist (I know no other
> word to use) finds hard to accept in a journalist.[13]

Hare has a particular objection to journalistic traditions being
applied to television drama (if in fact they are):

> Journalists have always been told that they must put up
> with having their work changed, for on a newspaper it is
> something which happens all the time. But in a theatre it
> never now happens, except by consent.[14]

But watching a television drama at home is not the same
experience as going to the theatre. Television and stage plays
are different creatures, they are made in different ways and
the same rules cannot apply to both. The playwright has not
got a divine right to airtime and an untouchable freedom to use
whatever obscenities and images he chooses without thought
of his audience, and playwrights who shriek neurotically
when one of many swear words in a script is cut rarely serve
the cause of quality drama. The creation of a television play is
a corporate act, and dramatists, along with others involved in
its making cannot ignore the fact that there are responsibilities
involved in mass communication. If the writer wilfully ignores
those responsibilities, then editorial (or production) control
may prove necessary.

However, where David Hare is right (and it must be
stressed that this is the main point of his essay) is when he
warns of blandness. As John Bowen pointed out, when reviewing the book in which Hare's essay was published:

Television can corrupt . . . by being always the same, by
avoiding what is upsetting – avoiding challenge, in fact, and
therefore the possibility of response – by avoiding all those
areas of moral choice with which drama is particularly
concerned.[15]

By applauding that opinion, I am not reneging on a previous
point and advocating unrestrained obscenities and violence.
Rather, to maintain Shaun Sutton's metaphor, I would argue
that it is a very dull guest who does not bring new ideas on a
visit and it is no business of a production house to restrict the
range of guests the viewer might allow into his home. Blandness is an ever-present trap for producers, especially those
prone to lose their nerve. Advertisers wanting something safe,
pressure groups that might cause a row and politicians can all
make life 'difficult' for producers and their management and
so encourage excessive caution, a caution urged by the generally supportive IBA *Guidelines* (despite that publication's
belief that 'drama is by definition the personal view of the
dramatist' and that 'the due impartiality required of a play by
an independent dramatist is not identical to that required of a
current affairs programme produced by a company's own
production team':

> The Authority believes that each case should be treated
> separately on its merits; but it would be unlikely to approve
> the scheduling of a play commending one side or the other in
> a matter of public policy, such as abortion, or capital
> punishment, at a time when that issue was being debated in
> Parliament, or of a play which took sides on any aspect of
> industrial relations during a strike of national importance.
> The Authority would also find considerable difficulty in
> agreeing to a series of single plays or a succession of drama
> series, all of which consistently took the same lines on
> contemporary issues, without any internal balance. And it
> would not accept any drama that was clearly designed to
> serve the interests of one political party.[16]

What would be frightening is a situation where plays about
abortion, capital punishment or political issues could never be
made and shown. The exploration of public issues and the

articulation of varied opinions, the presentation of new ideas are what television drama is uniquely well equipped to do, and the best playwrights (and directors and producers) can do that without causing the viewer in his or her front room to reach for the on—off button or remote-control channel changer. After all, the makers of a play presumably want an audience and one that consists of more than those whose job it is to watch.

The Critic

Television drama has not been well served by those whose job it is to watch plays and to assess them in them in the daily and weekly press. Press critics are of course in a strange position, because traditionally most press criticism of television drama (as of other types of programming) has appeared after a production's single showing in columns headed 'Last Night in View' or 'Last Week on the Box'. Although it must be very satisfying to those who have been involved in the making of a production to see it taken note of in the permanence of print, and although it is useful to the BBC and other production companies to have reviews from which they can select the odd gem-ette with which to plug a play either at the time of a repeat in eighteen months time or in the overseas sales catalogues, what use is such criticism to the reader of the paper (and/or viewer)?

I suspect that many newspaper readers skim television-review columns and read only those sections that cover prog-rammes they have seen: then it is agreeable to see what someone else thought of the show they spent an hour watching the night before. Therefore perhaps it is the desire to be read more thoroughly that has prompted several critics to develop an idiosyncratic style of writing that is far removed from genuine criticism (be it popular or academic). Such critics produce columns (often very funny ones) which are no more than comic essays written at the expense of television, columns where plays and other programmes have their content parodied but are not assessed.

In recent years there has been a welcome move towards the previewing of programmes: television production houses ar-range special screenings (often in rather plush, large-screen viewing-theatres) of forthcoming programmes. Sometimes these result in 'advance' critical pieces which encourage or illuminate the viewing of a particular production. Too often they generate publicity articles centred on a star performer. More useful have been the number of critical guides to 'the week ahead' which various papers (such as *The Sunday Times* and *Time Out*) have carried, but these columns have been limited by the copyright in programme details which has long been held by the publishers of *Radio Times* and *TV Times*, the 'official' programme journals.

In defence of the critics, it can be said that, while the range of television output is prodigious, newspapers still expect the critic to turn in 400 words one day on a science documentary, the next on an opera, the revamped news magazine or a play. At the same time they would think it grotesque or irresponsible to expect their science reporter to review a Covent Garden opera or even their opera critic to cover a play at the Barbican. In an important article, 'Reviewing the Critics', in which he bade farewell to television-reviewing before returning to production, W. Stephen Gilbert proposed one solution:

I can't see that it would be excessive for the quality papers to carry a family television page as well as an arts page with a staff as extensive as that covering the arts. It's absurd that the assessment of television runs at about the same wordage as the assessment of theatre. By any measure except the most impossibly elitist, television is hugely more important than the theatre – and I say that as someone who goes to the theatre on average twice a week. Yet, as Frank Marcus once pointed out, his first televised play, *The Window*, was 'almost totally ignored by the critics'. The same play was mounted for a fortnight a couple of years later in 'a restaurant basement' in Queensway whose maximum seating capacity was 35. 'Yet columns of reviews appeared in the press; it was even discussed on the BBC Overseas Service. As a result, it was published here and in America and has been performed extensively ever since.'[17]

Were such teams of critics as Gilbert envisages ever to be commonplace, it would be necessary for them to be educated in the crafts and arts of television – and especially in those of television drama. With one or two notable exceptions (such as Peter Fiddick), the technical appreciation of most press critics is alarmingly low. On the rare occasions when I have been in a television gallery and a press critic has been present, I have been surprised and saddened at his ignorance of the grammar of television and readiness that it should remain 'magic'.

For its own good, television drama (be it soap or the single play) needs informed criticism: criticism that educates the viewer, encourages discriminatory viewing and keeps practioners and managements on their toes. As W. Stephen Gilbert said in the same article, 'Television will grow up when it has generated a substantial body of serious assessment of itself. That daily it is still treated like a rather uncouth brat is seriously holding back its potential.'

The Student

Television drama deserves its students and enthusiasts.

It is a vast creative enterprise; an intrusive but popular power in the land. It is also vulnerable, subject to the forces of commerce and reaction, the constant prey of such beasts as complacency and caution.

Television drama needs its students and enthusiasts. In a world where 'wide appeal' can all too easily be taken to mean 'excellent' and where 'popular' can become a synonym for 'bland', space, time and money must be kept for original and quality drama (be it of mass appeal or not). The innovative and the challenging play, indeed the very form of the single television play, needs all the support that can be mustered.

That said, it must be stressed that television is a part of daily life and its students, while learning to read it critically and appreciatively, must understand it for what it is, as well as for what it might be. Its cause is not helped by those who scorn a series or a serial simply because it is popular. There is much merit in a plain tale well told, and it is as easy to be snobbish about a well-crafted play simply because it is about, say, detection or romance, as it is for the literary critic to be snobbish about a television play because it is not a stage play.

However much we might wish it to be an educative influence, we must always remember that television drama is nothing if it does not entertain.

Glossary

A guide to some of the less arcane and politer words used in the making of television drama.

all film job	drama made entirely on film
assembly	rough putting-together of film or tape in script order; fine editing has yet to be done (see p. 137)
assistant-cameraman	assistant to chief or lighting camera-man (loads film, may alter focus, operate clapperboard, etc.)
banner title	title for series of single plays; also *umbrella title*
barn doors	see p. 133.
blockbuster	programme intended to win massive audience
boom	telescopic arm for directing and sus-pending microphones
box	see *gallery*
cable TV	television distributed by cables
can	round metal box holding reels of film; hence 'in the can' (it's finished)
cans	headphones
catwalk	high-level walkway used to give access to lighting-*grid*
cherrypicker	hydraulically operated tower for high-angle camera work
chippy	carpenter
Chroma Key	see p. 115
clapperboard	hinged board on which are chalked details of each film take (see pp. 120 and 137)

clip	short film sequence
CSO	see p. 115
crab	to move the camera sideways
credits	lists of actors, artists, crew taking part in production, shown on screen
crew	term for personnel involved in programme other than those who appear on screen
cut	(1) director's order to stop filming; (2) to switch from one camera to another; (3) to edit film
day for night	filming night time scenes during the day, by using special lens filters (and special printing-techniques)
DBS	direct broadcasting by satellite
dress	to prepare a set by adding furniture, curtains, etc.
dub	to add sound to tape or film
dubbing mixer	technician responsible for dubbing
effects bank	panel of switches, buttons, etc., used by vision mixer
EFP	electronic field production, a similar technique to ENG (q.v.)
ENG	electronic news-gathering; the use of lightweight, portable video cameras on location
flashback	dramatic scene which relates earlier part of the plot
fold back	pre-recorded sound played to studio floor
fourth wall	the imaginary wall of a set, never seen by viewers
frame	one individual film picture
gaffer	chief electrician
gallery	production control room; sometimes called the 'box'
gate	part of film camera or projector in which each frame of the film is momentarily held as it is photographing or being played back

grid	network of metal piping from which lamps are hung in a studio
grip	man who serves film crews by laying tracks; sometimes by moving cables
i. p. s.	inches per second (for measuring tape speed)
lighting-cameraman	leading cameraman of film unit
line-up	period of studio time for adjusting equipment before recording starts
mute	film without sound
pan	to move camera in a horizontal plane
programme ident	identifying number at the start of a video programme
props	objects used to dress a set; action props are ones used by actors (e.g. telephone)
punch up	to switch a camera or telecine or a caption into transmission mode
racks	the studio department responsible for picture quality
radio mike	performer's microphone which transmits sound to a nearby receiver and which needs no cable
rig	to set up equipment and lights
rushes	sequences of film processed overnight
scanner	mobile control room
scenery dock	area for storing scenery
sparks	electrician
spot effect	sound effect created in studio
stagehand	member of studio-floor crew who rigs and clears the set
telecine	process of converting film to video
television novel	epic serial written for television (not adapted from a novel but might be turned into one)
tilt	to move a camera in the vertical plane
track	to move a camera to follow an actor
umbrella title	see *banner title*
unit manager	on location, the person responsible for catering, transport, etc.

whip pan	very fast *pan*
zoom	use of zoom lens on camera (see p. 132)
zoom happy	too much use of the *zoom*

Common Abbreviations Used in Camera Scripts

BCU	big close-up: showing head or part of the head
CU	close-up: showing head and shoulders
MCU	medium close-up: showing subject just above waist
CMS	close medium shot: cutting the subject below the waist
MS	medium shot: cutting subject at the knees
MLS	medium long shot: showing full-length figure
LS	long shot: figure about half height of the screen
VLS	very long shot: showing full set
AB	as before: camera has exactly the same shot as immediately before
cam	camera
F/X	sound effects on tape or disc
grams	music or sound effects from gramophone records
mic	microphone
OOV	out of vision: speech, music, effects heard but source unseen
POV	point of view (e.g. Charley's POV)
SOF	sound on film
super	superimpose (usually titles or credits on a background picture)
VTR	video-tape recording
V/O	voice-over (see p. 93)

Notes and References

1. Genres and Media

1. Hugh Whitemore, 'Word into Image: Reflections on Television Dramatisation', in *Ah! Mischief: The Writer and Television*, ed. F. Pike (London: Faber & Faber, 1982) p. 101.

2. W. Stephen Gilbert, 'The Television Play: Outside the Consensus', *Screen Education*, no. 35 (Summer 1980) p. 35.

3. Graham Murdock, 'Authorship and Organisation', ibid., p. 29.

4. Peter Buckman, 'Illuminations', *The Listener*, 19 April, 1979, pp. 554–5.

5. Shaun Sutton, *The Largest Theatre in the World* (London: BBC, 1982) p. 20.

6. Barry Hanson, in 'The Rise and Fall of the Single Play', London Weekend Television, 8 April 1979.

7. Robert Holles, 'Independent Television and the Single Play' paper delivered to the Society of Authors, 1979.

8. David Reid, 'The Single Play', in *Television and Radio 1980* (London: IBA, 1980) p. 25.

9. John Bowen, 'Protecting the Public Story-tellers', *The Times Educational Supplement*, 21 May 1982, p. 26.

10. Michael Bakewell, 'The Television Production', in *The Wars of the Roses* (London: BBC, 1970) pp. 233–4.

11. Jonathan Raban, '*Leeds – United!*: Drama Making News', *Radio Times*, 7 November 1974, p. 82.

12. Paul Johnson, 'Journalists as Play Actors', *The Listener*, 19 March 1981, pp. 362–3.

13. Robin Sutch, 'Reality Principle', *Guardian*, 26 August 1980, p. 7.

14. Raban, in *Radio Times*, 7 November 1974, p. 82.
15. Joseph Hone, 'Saints and Sinners', *The Listener*, 14 September 1978, p. 341.
16. David Wheeler, 'Faultless Faction', *The Listener*, 10 September 1981, p. 282.
17. David Edgar, 'Documentary Drama', in *Ah! Mischief*, ed. Pike, p. 20.
18. John Ellis, *Visible Fictions* (London: Routledge & Kegan Paul, 1982) pp. 121ff. and 145ff.
19. *Television and Radio 1983* (London: IBA, 1983) pp. 60–1.
20. Patrick Stoddard, 'Soldiering: A Serious Business', *Broadcast*, 28 February 1983, p. 22.
21. John Naughton, 'Visual Feasts', *The Listener*, 15 October 1981, p. 446.
22. Sutton, *The Largest Theatre in the World*, p. 37.
23. MP, 'Co-produced Lawrence', *The Listener*, 3 February 1983, p. 33.
24. Naughton, in *The Listener*, 15 October 1981, p. 446.
25. Peter Fiddick, 'Soap Operas', *Guardian*, 15 April 1980, Arts page.
26. Peter Buckman, 'In Praise of Soaps', *The Listener*, 19 August 1982, pp. 25–6.
27. Ibid.
28. David Hare, 'Ah! Mischief: The Rule of Public Broadcasting', in *Ah! Mischief*, ed. Pike, p. 47.

2. The Providers

1. *BBC Year Book 1947* (London: BBC, 1947) p. 79.
2. John Swift, *Adventure in Vision* (London: John Lehmann, 1950).
3. Shaun Sutton, 1981 Fleming Memorial Lecture, given at the Royal Institution, 2 April 1981.
4. Bernard Sendall, *Independent Television in Britain*, vol. 1 (Macmillan, 1982) pp. 345–6, 338–9.
5. *The First Twenty One Years* (Norwich: Anglia Television, 1980) p. 71.
6. Nick Elliot, quoted in Karen Margolis, 'Gong et Lumière', *Broadcast*, 31 January 1983 (Monte Carlo Supplement).

7. David Cunliffe, ibid.
8. Margaret Matheson, ibid.
9. Sutton, 1981 Fleming Memorial Lecture.

3. The Producer
1. Richard Paterson, 'The Production Context of *Coronation Street*', in Richard Dyer *et al.*, *Coronation Street*, BFI TV Monograph no. 13 (London: British Film Institute, 1981) p. 57.
2. Anthony Smith, 'The Relationship of Management with Creative Staff', in Lord Annan (Chairman), *Report of the Committee on the Future of Broadcasting* (London: Her Majesty's Stationery Office, 1977).

4. The Writer
1. John Wyver, 'The Great Authorship Mystery', *The Listener*, 14 April 1983, p. 36.
2. Julian Mitchell, 'Television: An Outsider's View', in *Ah! Mischief*, ed. Pike, pp. 54–5.
3. C. P. Taylor, *Making a TV Play* (Newcastle upon Tyne: Oriel Press, 1970) pp. 17–18.
4. David Cook, 'Writing Plays for Television', in *Broadcasting Bulletin* (Society of Authors), November 1981, p. 12.
5. Mitchell, in *Ah! Mischief*, ed. Pike, pp. 54–5.
6. Sir Huw Wheldon, The Richard Dimbleby Lecture 1976, *The Listener*, 4 March 1976, pp. 265–7.
7. Mitchell, in *Ah! Mischief*, ed. Pike, pp. 54–5.

5. The Director
1. John Challen, *Lifelike*, BBC Television play.
2. Tristan de Vere Cole, 'Director's Notes,' in Taylor, *Making a TV Play,* pp. 74–5.
3. Paterson, 'The Production Context of *Coronation Street*', in Dyer *et al.*, *Coronation Street*, pp. 58–9.

6. The Cast
1. Hare, 'Ah! Mischief: The Role of Public Broadcasting', in *Ah! Mischief*, ed. Pike, p. 47.
2. Sutton, *The Largest Theatre in the World*, p. 109.

3. Michael Billington, 'Acting Observant', *Radio Times*, 16–22 October 1982, p. 8.
4. John Gielgud, *An Actor and his Time* (London: Sidgwick & Jackson, 1979).
5. Clive Swift, *The Job of Acting* (London: Harrap, 1976) p. 77.
6. Gielgud, *An Actor and his Time*.

7. **Design**
1. Richard Levin, 'Scene in Colour', in *BBC Handbook 1968* (London: BBC, 1968) pp. 12–13.
2. Harry Fenwick, 'The Production', in *The Tempest*, The BBC Television Shakespeare (London: BBC, 1980) p. 18.
3. Gerald Millerson, *Basic TV Staging*, 2nd edn (London and Boston, Mass.: Focal Press, 1982) p. 12.

8. **On Location**
1. Michael Bakewell, 'The Television Production', in *The Wars of the Roses* (London: BBC, 1970) p. 232.
2. Michael Simpson, 'Directing Break In', in *Scene Scripts Two*, Longman Imprint Books (London: Longman, 1978) p. 104.
3. Christopher Griffin-Beale, 'BBC Pushes Boat Out', *Broadcast*, 30 March 1981, p. 22.
4. David Foster, 'The Play's the Thing', *Broadcast*, 14 March 1983, p. 13.
5. Glyn Alkin, *TV Sound Operations* (London: Focal Press, 1975) p. 120.

9. **In the Studio**
1. Marta Wöhrle, 'Europe's Fastest Production Unit', *Broadcast*, 21 October 1983, p. 26.
2. John Glenister, in 'Behind the Scenes with . . .', BBC-1, 5 November 1981.
3. Alkin, *TV Sound Operations*, p. 50.

10. **Post-production**
1. Robin Shenfield, 'Off-line on Offer: VT Editing

Facts' in *Broadcast*, 27 June 1983 (Video-tape Editing Supplement).
  2. Geoff Posner, ibid.
  3. Jim Baler, ibid.
  4. Brian Eastman, ibid.
  5. Shenfield, ibid.
  6. Martin Hicks, ibid.
  7. Terry Dennell, ibid.

11. **The Audience**
  1. Ellis, *Visible Fictions*, p. 167.
  2. Sutton, *The Largest Theatre in the World*, p. 131.
  3. Ibid.
  4. Ellis, *Visible Fictions*, p. 167.
  5. Independent Broadcasting Authority, *Television Programme Guidelines* (London: IBA, 1979) pp. 1–2.
  6. Ibid.
  7. *British Television Drama*, ed. George W. Brandt (London and Cambridge: Cambridge University Press, 1981) p. 31.
  8. H. J. Eysenck and D. K. B. Nias, *Sex, Violence and the Media* (London: Temple Smith, 1978) p. 274.
  9. IBA, *Television Programme Guidelines*, p. 1.
  10. Ibid., p. 24.
  11. Sutton, *The Largest Theatre in the World*, p. 133.
  12. Ibid., p. 131.
  13. Hare, 'Ah! Mischief: The Role of Public Broadcasting', in *Ah! Mischief*, ed. Pike, p. 42.
  14. Ibid., p. 43.
  15. John Bowen, 'Protecting the Public Story-tellers', *The Times Educational Supplement*, 21 May 1982, p. 26.
  16. IBA, *Television Programme Guidelines*, p. 6.
  17. W. Stephen Gilbert, 'Reviewing the Critics', *Broadcast*, 5 July 1982, pp. 12–13.

Select Bibliography

Ah! Mischief: The Writer and Television, ed. Frank Pike (London: Faber & Faber, 1982).

ALKIN, GLYN, *TV Sound Operations* (London: Focal Press, 1975).

ALVARDO, MANUEL, and BUSCOMBE, EDWARD, *Hazell – the Making of a TV Series* (London: British Film Institute in association with Latimer, 1982).

British Television Drama, ed. George W. Brandt (London and Cambridge: Cambridge University Press, 1981).

DYER, RICHARD, *et al.*, *Coronation Street*, BFI TV Monograph no. 13 (London: British Film Institute, 1981).

ELLIS, JOHN, *Visible Fictions* (London: Routledge & Kegan Paul, 1982).

Focal Encyclopedia of Film and Television Techniques, ed. Raymond Spottiswoode (London and Boston, Mass.: Focal Press, 1969).

MILLERSON, GERALD, *Basic TV Staging*, 2nd edn (London & Boston, Mass.: Focal Press, 1982).

—— *TV Lighting Methods*, 2nd edn (London & Boston, Mass.: Focal Press, 1982).

SHUBIK, IRENE, *Play for Today: The Evolution of Television Drama* (London: Davies-Poynter, 1975).

SUTTON, SHAUN, *The Largest Theatre in the World* (London: BBC, 1982).

TAYLOR, C. P., *Making a Television Play* (Newcastle upon Tyne: Oriel Press, 1970).

WILKIE, BERNARD, *Creating Special Effects for TV and Films* (London and Boston, Mass.: Focal Press, 1977).

WILLIAMS, RAYMOND, *Television, Technology and Cultural Form* (London: Fontana, 1974).

—— *Drama in a Dramatised Society: An Inaugural Lecture* (London and Cambridge: Cambridge University Press, 1975).

Index